The Voice of Black Theology in South Africa

Louise Kretzschmar

Ravan Press
Johannesburg

To David and Rhoda

Published by Ravan Press (Pty) Ltd
P O Box 31134, Braamfontein, 2017 South Africa

©Copyright Louise Kretzschmar 1986

First impression 1986

ISBN 0 86975 269 3

Cover Design: New Art
Set in 9 on 10pt Sabon/Symposia

Printed and bound by Sigma Press (Pty) Ltd, Pretoria

Contents

Abbreviations   vii
Preface   ix

INTRODUCTION   xi

CHAPTER ONE: The Rise of South African Black Theology   1
    Three Christian Leaders
    Black Christian Leaders and South African Society
    Black Leaders and Christianity

CHAPTER TWO: The Broader Theological Context   14
    African Theology
    Black Theology in the USA
    Latin American Liberation Theology

CHAPTER THREE: The Africanisation of Christianity   24
    Christianity and African Traditional Religion
    Christian Faith and African Ancestors
    Christianity and African Culture
    African Theology and Political Issues

CHAPTER FOUR: The African Independent (Indigenous) Churches   43
    The 19th Century Establishment of the AICs
    The Phenomenal Growth of the AICs
    The Contribution of the AICs
    The AICs and Social Transformation

CHAPTER FIVE: Black Theology and Black Identity   58
    The Rise of Black Consciousness
    The Relationship between Black Consciousness and Black Theology
    Blackness, Racism and Integration
    Black Theology, Black Nationalism and Liberation

CHAPTER SIX: Black Liberation and Black Theology   71
    What is Hermeneutics?
    The Meaning of Liberation and the Identity of the Poor
    Liberation Theology and the Church
    Some Concluding Comments

CHAPTER SEVEN: White Theological Responses to Apartheid   94
                Ideology and Black Theology
    White Theological Critiques of Civil Religion and Apartheid
    The Reaction to the Growth of Black Theology
    Liberation and the Church

CONCLUSION   110

Bibliography   116
Index   135

Abbreviations

Journals

BibSacra	*Bibliotheca Sacra*
ComVia	*Communio Viatorium*
Ecunews	*Ecumenical News*
EcuR	*Evangelical Review of Theology*
EvRT	*Evangelical Review of Theology*
HTR	*Harvard Theological Review*
IRM	*International Review of Mission*
JAS	*Journal of African Studies*
JRA	*Journal of Religion in Africa*
JSSR	*Journal for the Scientific Study of Religion*
JTSA	*Journal of Theology for Southern Africa*
Miss	*Missionalia*
Missiology	*Missiology: An International Review*
NGTT	*Nederduitse Gereformeerde Teologiese Tydskrif*
ProV	*Pro Veritate*
RvEx	*Review and Expositor*
SAO	*South African Outlook*
ThFB	*Theological Fraternity Bulletin*
TVia	*Theologica Viatorum*

Other Abbreviations

AAC	All-African Convention
AACC	All Africa Conference of Churches
AICs	African Independent Churches

ANC	African National Congress
ASATI	Association of Southern African Theological Institutes
ASSECA	Association for the Educational, Social and Cultural Advancement of African People in South Africa
ET	English Translation
CCSA	Christian Council of South Africa
CI	Christian Institute of Southern Africa
GK	Gereformeerde Kerk
IDAMASA	Interdenominational African Ministers' Association of South Africa
NCBC	National Congress of Black Churchmen
NGK	Nederduitse Gereformeerde Kerk
NGKA	Nederduitse Gereformeerde Kerk in Afrika
NGSK/Sendingkerk	Nederduitse Gereformeerde Sendingkerk
NHK	Nederduitse Hervormde Kerk
NUSAS	National Union of South African Students
PAC	Pan Africanist Congress
RCA	Reformed Church in Africa
SACC	South African Council of Churches
SASO	South African Student Organisation
Spro-cas	Study Project on Christianity in Apartheid Society
UCM	University Christian Movement
UNISA	University of South Africa
UP	University Press
WARC	World Alliance of Reformed Churches

Preface

This book would never have been started without my interaction with the many theologians under whom I have been able to study, or whose books I have read. I wish, therefore, to thank individuals such as Professors Ben Engelbrecht (University of the Witwatersrand), Adrian Hastings (University of Aberdeen and now Zimbabwe), David Bosch (University of South Africa) and John de Gruchy (University of Cape Town). There are many others whom I cannot mention here, with whom I have come into contact, directly or indirectly, both in South Africa and abroad, to whom thanks are due. Responsibility for any misunderstandings or weaknesses, however, can certainly not be laid at their door.

The book, having been begun, would never have been completed without the encouragement and support of many others. Among these I would like to mention two of my colleagues at the University of Transkei, Professor Ephraim Mosothoane and Canon Luke Pato. Also, gratitude and thanks are extended to my late father David, my mother Rhoda Kretzschmar, and to June, Edward, and Berendien, for their continued love and support. In addition, I would like to express appreciation for the encouragement and practical assistance of my friends in Umtata, especially that of Philip and Friedmann.

Ms Mkhize greatly assisted me in reducing mountains of scribbled notes to computer print-outs and Ms Msomi worked with me in preparing the index. Finally, I thank my editor, Peter Randall, for his invaluable help in preparing the manuscript for publication.

Introduction

Since the early days of the penetration of Christianity into South Africa, Africans, and subsequently 'Coloureds' and 'Indians', have responded to the message of the Gospel. Thus it is today, that the Christian churches in South Africa have several million black members. This fact alone should indicate that the theological understanding and church practices of these believers are extremely significant for Christianity in South Africa.

In recent years, interest in South African Black Theology (by which I mean the theological writings of black South African Christians) has become increasingly apparent. No doubt this is largely because of the growing numbers of articulate black theologians, as well as statements by prominent and controversial churchmen such as Bishop Desmond Tutu and Dr Allan Boesak. These more recent developments, however, should not obscure the fact that the Black Theology of the 1970s and 80s has, as its historical context, the black Christian experience and witness of previous centuries. In this book, however, I have restricted myself largely to the 20th century and especially to the developments of the last two decades during which the voice of Black Christianity has presented us all with criticisms and challenges. It is a voice that must not be ignored or silenced.

My own interst in South African Black Theology was first awakened nearly ten years ago, by contact with black Christians during my student years and, subsequently, by my reading of the Black Theology that had emerged from the USA. Serious study of the subject was begun only in 1980, as part of a postgraduate theology degree in England. During this time, I realised that there were several black South Africans who were seeking to write theology that was meaningful within their life-experience. In addition, I came increasingly to realise that they were, in many ways, echoing earlier voices. This book is a result of my pursuit of the thoughts, experiences and writings of the black Christian prophets of South Africa.

Naturally, given the unavoidable delays in publication, a study of Black Theology in South Africa cannot be completely up to date. This study does not venture much beyond the early 1980s and, therefore, many of the more recent statements and activities of individuals such as Bishop Tutu and Dr Boesak could not be discussed.

No book can contain all the available information on a particular subject. Therefore, I have sought to select what I regard to be important personalities, books and themes, and to provide the reader with an introduction to, what could be broadly termed, South African Black Theology. Black Theology, then, is the theological response of blacks to the Christian Gospel. Within this three broad themes are found.

a) African Theology, which emphasises the relationship between Christianity and African traditional religion and culture.

b) Black Theology as Black Consciousness, ie those writings which emphasise that blackness is not to be negated as inferior, but affirmed as part of God's creation, and which draws out the implications of a Black Theology for the Church.

c) Black Theology as Liberation Theology which stresses that the Gospel is a Gospel of liberation — a liberation of individuals from the oppressive social structures in which they live and the creation of a new society.

Individual black theologians may, as Desmond Tutu does, embrace all three of these. Others, such as Allan Boesak, emphasise Black Consciousness and Liberation, while yet others, like Gabriel Setiloane, will speak mainly in terms of African Theology. South African Black Theology is thus an umbrella term, which seeks to draw together the various concerns of black South African theologians.

In chapter one I seek to show that many early 20th century African leaders were men of Christian conviction who spoke out not only on narrowly 'religious' issues, but also about the society which so often called itself Christian, whilst failing desperately to live up to the Gospel it preached. Chapter two indicates the broader international theological context of South African Black Theology. The theology emerging from the African continent is briefly discussed, together with the Black Theology of the USA and Latin American Liberation Theology. Chapters three and four examine the Africanisation of Christianity. In chapters five and six I discuss the political implications of the Christian faith. Finally, in chapter seven, various responses to South African Black Theology are described and analysed.

Before commencing this examination, some remarks regarding terminology and methodology are in order. Following general usage, I have avoided terms such as 'Native', 'Non-European' and 'Bantu' (unless the context demands them), preferring to speak of Africans. Unfortunately the terms 'Coloured' and

'Indian' seem to be unavoidable. All these groups are then collectively termed black, rather than 'non-white'.

I have attempted, as much as possible, to allow black theologians and church leaders to speak for themselves and have included several quotations from their writings. Obviously, because I place their words in a structure of my own making, personal interpretation intrudes, but I hope that this does not amount to misinterpretation or distortion. My purpose throughout is to make it possible for the non-specialist reader to encounter a broad range of black opinion within the Church in South Africa. Fairly extensive footnotes are provided for those readers who wish to obtain more detailed information.

It will also be evident that I have sought to assess Black Theology in terms of its claim to be a biblical theology. This would seem to be justifiable on the basis of the fact that these black theologians have concentrated, not on questioning the authority or value of the Bible, but rather on questioning many traditional (white) interpretations of the text and on developing a new way of interpreting the Bible.

This book is necessary, I believe, because although there are a great many articles on Black Theology, most of these are in theological journals, which are not usually read by the public or even by church members. Moreover, although in recent years books have been published by black South African theologians, there is a need for a general introduction to some of their writings. Whilst this book is largely descriptive, I have also introduced, where relevant, the ideas of others and, indeed, my own responses. This is necessary in order to pursue the task of developing a theology that speaks in a meaningful and challenging way. I am not black, and do not claim to have either plumbed the depths of black South African experience and thought, or to have pronounced the last word on South African Black Theology. But I trust that this book will inform and stimulate others to engage in a discussion of the concerns and criticisms that it raises.

CHAPTER ONE

The Rise of South African Black Theology

Black Christians have long been speaking out concerning the church and related socio-economic and political issues. Although the terms African Theology, Black Theology and Liberation Theology have only been in use relatively recently, many of the major concerns of these theologies have been expressed in the past. This means that 'South African Black Theology' dates back earlier than the 1970s and that the voices of black Christians have not previously been silent. It also means that today's Christians, and especially white believers, should become more aware of, and also respond to, these prophetic voices.

It is not possible here to give a detailed examination of the initial responses of blacks to Christian mission[1]. It is necessary, however, to briefly point out certain aspects of the legacy of the previous two centuries, a legacy that did much to set the tone for the 20th century Christian experience in South Africa.

The early missionaries, especially in the 19th century, are to be commended for sowing the seed from which the black churches of the 20th century grew. They did extensive evangelistic work, built churches, schools and hospitals. Not only were these important aspects of their ministries at that time, but were also to serve as significant foundations for subsequent developments. This is seen, for example, in such schools as Lovedale and Healdtown (Cape) and Adams College (Natal) which were attended by many blacks who were to become leaders. Thus,

> . . . whatever the faults of the missionaries, from a black as well as a white perspective, it is true to say that the church's struggle against racism and injustice in South Africa only really begins in earnest with their witness in the nineteenth century.[2]

Another important legacy of the 19th century was the formation of the African Independent Churches. As these are discussed in chapter four, I need at this point merely to mention that the earliest secessions began in the 1870s and that, in terms of both number and influence, the AICs were to grow at a phenomenal rate. Moreover, they were an early indication of dissatisfaction with the white domination of the churches and of a desire to express the Christian faith in ways that were compatible with African traditional life.

By the end of the 19th century, then, black Christians were members of either the mission churches (Anglican, Methodist, Baptist, etc) or of the African Independent churches. In the former, the higher positions of leadership were almost exclusively in the hands of whites, while the latter were founded and led by blacks. Although churches (such as the Anglican) provided programmes of training and ordination for blacks, the role of blacks was largely limited to local parishes. During the first half of the 20th century no black Anglican bishops were appointed.

In the mission churches paternalism was rife, and blacks were regarded more as children in the faith than as partners in ministry. The thinking and ministry of these churches was determined by white interpretations and decisions. As a result, such features as African worship, culture and beliefs were ignored or dismissed, rather than adopted and Christianised. In fact, it was for these three reasons (lack of leadership opportunity, paternalism and failure to deal fairly with the world views and customs of Africans) more than any other, that many black Christians broke away to form their own churches.

In the Dutch Reformed Churches, many of the above attitudes were also prevalent. What is more, a decision of the DRC (NGK) Synod in 1857, which had been intended as a temporary measure, had become a rule:

> The Synod considers it desirable and scriptural that our members from the Heathen be received and absorbed into our existing congregations wherever possible; but where this measure, as a result of the weakness of some, impedes the furtherance of the cause of Christ among the Heathen, the congregation from the Heathen, already founded or still to be founded, shall enjoy its Christian privileges in a separate building or institution.[3]

It was the consistent application of separate worship and association that led to the subsequent establishment of the *Sendingkerk* or NGSK (for Coloureds) in 1881, the *NG Kerk in Afrika* or NGKA (for Africans) and the (Indian) Reformed Church of Africa (RCA).

By the start of this century, the South African pattern of political domination and socio-economic privilege had pretty much imposed itself on the Church. Notions of white supremacy took the place of mutual respect and affection. Separation and exclusivism replaced fellowship and community spirit. Racism had penetrated the faith.

There were individuals or even certain churches who did not fit into this mould. But the general state of affairs and the patterns of future developments had been indicated. This general description does not deny that there were major educational and cultural differences between different groups which were obstacles to easy assimilation. What must be noted is the inclination of the Christian Church to follow the pattern of the world rather than of the Scriptures, and, in so doing, to incapacitate itself so that it was less and less able to be a witness to the world. Instead of being the leaven, salt and light in the South African context, the Churches, in terms of both ideology and practice, became practically inseparable from it.

It is against this background that the thinking and activities of black Christians in the earlier part of the 20th century should be examined. In this examination two broad issues will be raised. Firstly, the nature of black Christian leadership in society as a whole, and secondly black leadership in the churches.

Three Christian Leaders

It is clear that black Christian leaders were at the forefront of African nationalist movements. In the same way that the NG Kerk was later to initiate and support Afrikaner nationalism, work for the improvement of the Afrikaners' lifestyle and promote their quest for political power, Christian African leaders sought to lead their own people:

> . . . it is obvious that much of the leadership of the black nationalist movement was Christian, and that many of the leaders were ministers within the mission and English-speaking churches. Virtually all the leaders were trained and educated at missionary institutions, and their petitions and protests stress the fact that their motivation stemmed from Christian principles and convictions. African nationalism depended heavily on educated Christian leadership.[4]

The significance of this group of people can hardly be over-estimated. For the purposes of this discussion, three examples will have to suffice. These are Jabavu, Matthews and Luthuli.[5]

DDT Jabavu, like his father, John Tengo Jabavu, was a black Christian leader of great stature. Born in 1885, he studied in South Africa and abroad. By 1916 he was a lecturer at Fort Hare University. After lecturing in African languages, anthropology, history and Latin, he was made a professor. During a long and active public life, he gave speeches, formed and joined societies and wrote pamphlets. He gave both time and effort to matters educational, religious and political. He was also for many years an active leader in the AAC (All-African Convention) and was repeatedly involved in representations to the government to promote African political rights. He was a gradualist who believed that Christian morality would eventually compel whites to extend the qualified Cape franchise to other provinces, and even move beyond this to an unqualified and equal vote. In this he was to be proved wrong. For, from 1936 onwards, those few blacks who qualified were first removed from the common voters roll and then denied the limited parliamentary representation they had previously received through separately elected (white) senators. It should come as no surprise, therefore, that later generations of young black leaders were to look back at Jabavu, and others like him, and question the value not only of their dedication to peace and gradualism (or evolutionary development) but also to Christianity.

ZK (Zachariah Keodirelang) Matthews, born in Kimberley in 1901, was one of South Africa's most distinguished black academics. He was the first black BA graduate in South Africa (Fort Hare, 1923) and the first to receive an LLB (1930). He received an MA from Yale University and in 1935 was appointed lecturer at Fort Hare. Subsequently, he became a professor and an important spokesman for blacks at home and abroad. A dedicated Anglican, he was active in the Natives' Representative Council (NRC) and the African National Congress (ANC).[6] He served also on missionary councils and worked towards better education for blacks. In 1959 he resigned from Fort Hare because of its take-over by the government and in 1961 became the secretary of the Africa section of the World Council of Churches (WCC). In 1966 he was appointed Botswana's representative at the United Nations. He died in 1968.

Albert John Luthuli (Lutuli) was born in 1898 in Rhodesia where his father was working as an evangelist. He later returned home with his mother to Groutville mission in Natal. Subsequently, he became a teacher, was confirmed in the Methodist Church and became a lay preacher. In 1920 he attended and later taught at Adams College. Later in life he spoke of his debt to the college:

> It became clear to me that the Christian faith was not a private affair without relevance to society. It was, rather, a belief which equipped us in a unique way to meet the challenges of our society. It was a belief which had to be applied to the conditions of our lives; and our many works — they ranged from Sunday School teaching to road building — became meaningful as the outflow of Christian belief.[7]

After 17 years at Adams College, in response to the pleading of his villagers, he again returned to Groutville and to the wife whom he had seen only intermittently for nearly two decades. He became a local chief and was immediately plunged into a broad range of activities on behalf of his people. These included matters such as law, agriculture, education, employment and health. It was, in fact, his experience as a chief that led him (at the age of 50) into politics, in an attempt to ameliorate the conditions under which blacks lived. And, in all of this, he sought to live out his Christian faith in an effective way.

He was involved with the ANC, first in Natal and then on a national level. He was active in the well organised and non-violent Defiance Campaign in 1952. By the end of that year he was elected president general of the ANC, only to be banned in 1953. Arrested at the time of the Treason Trials in 1956, he was released after preliminary examination. Even though he was intermittently banned thereafter, he continued to write speeches, address meetings and generally exercise extensive influence over the ANC. He was loved and revered by many, and feared by some. Throughout, he conducted himself with courage and integrity. In 1961 he was given permission to travel to Norway to receive the Nobel Peace Prize. He died in 1967.

Jabavu, Matthews and Luthuli then, serve as early examples of African Christian protest against a discriminating society.

The ANC was an important vehicle of expression for many early black leaders, Formed in 1912, the congress consistently included dedicated Christians amongst its leaders. The influence of the Christian men was evident not only in its formulations and aims but also in its methods. This may sound strange to modern ears, in the light of some of the present, more radical and violent, activities of the ANC. But this should not obscure the fact that the ANC began, and was for many years, an extremely moderate organisation — at least by modern standards. Its work proceeded in the form of speeches, letters, petitions, passive resistance and later non-violent boycotts. It sought to ensure a better future for the African people. The ANC petitioned the government time and time again either to change existing discriminatory legislation, or to halt proposed unjust legislation. It protested against the Land Act of 1913, the working and living conditions of Africans, their disenfranchisement and their lack of opportunity, educational and otherwise. From time to time it also co-operated with other groups, such as the Indian leaders, in an attempt to halt injustice, racism and suffering. Indeed it can be said that it was the continued intransigence of whites that was the major cause of the subsequent radicalisation of the ANC.

It is perhaps necessary here to reply to the often repeated assertions that religion and politics do not mix and that ministers of religion should not be involved in politics. Such statements, although they may appear to embody some wisdom, are both false and foolish, because religion, and especially Christianity, cannot be so easily divorced from life. Christian faith has a bearing on the life of the individual and therefore also upon his or her social context. Faced with the examples of God's interest in human affairs, and his use of prophets, kings and others to influence and even change their societies, Christians cannot be content with a gospel which is 'so heavenly minded that it is no earthly good'. The Christian faith is not, as the pietists would have us believe, simply a matter of the salvation of the indivdual's soul. If it were, the Bible would not have the emphasis it does on relationships, law and social behaviour. Believers have been commanded to live out and preach 'all that I have commanded you' in preparation for the consummation of the Kingdom of God and no Christian can, with biblical consistency, refuse to acknowledge his or her individual responsibility (and collectively that of the Church) to society.

If these are the principles on which Christian action in society is to be based, there is also the evidence of what has actually occurred in South African history. The liberal tradition, whatever its weaknesses, is closely associated with biblical notions of justice and human rights. Also, Afrikaner nationalism has made much use of the Old Testament notions of the purity and perpetuation of the nation.[8] The fact of the matter is that the Christian gospel has been used, and often distorted, for political ends. The only adequate response in such a situation is not withdrawal, but engagement. It is the responsibility of the church to be united, of one mind and purpose, and to stand as a living and serving witness to the whole world in general and South African society in particular.

Certainly, this was how many blacks viewed the task of the church, and for the African Christian leaders mentioned above religion could not be separated from life. The churches were called to support and further the cause of the homeless, landless and powerless.

Black Christian Leaders and South African Society

In analysing black political movements (in which Christians were involved) from the earliest days of the Union to the present, four major demands will be mentioned: the demands for land, socio-economic rights, educational opportunity and for full political representation.

In the negotiations surrounding the Union Constitution of 1910, Britain made little or no attempt to safeguard the rights of blacks in terms of political representation and land. Only in the Cape province did a qualified 'Native' franchise exist. The stage was set for the use of legislation to consolidate white ownership of *land,* much of which had previously been possessed by blacks, along the lines of Shepstone's policy of 'reserves' in Natal.

In 1913, the Native Land Act severely limited black opportunity to acquire land outside the reserves.[9] The dispossession of blacks was thus enforced by law, which meant, of course, that any attempt to have this process reversed would be regarded as subversive. Even under the present dispensation of the 'homelands' the amount of land set aside for blacks remains little changed, at about 13 per cent of South Africa's surface area.

Some churches spoke out in opposition to the 1913 Land Act. In 1915 the Anglican Church, for instance, stated that the Act should be 'immediately repealed until such time as more generous and comprehensive legislation is forthcoming'.[10] (Church opposition to other legislative acts was to increase as the years went by. This will be discussed in chapter seven.)

Both before and after Union in 1910, blacks petitioned the British and South African authorities on these issues, but to no avail. In the following decades these matters were to surface repeatedly as blacks attempted to break out of the stranglehold of general landlessness and their debilitating dependence on white farmers and, later, white-controlled industries and businesses.

There were other important *socio-economic* areas of injustice and dissatisfaction. As the years passed blacks found that they were expected to continue to accept inadequate houses, low wages and discrimination in employment. They had little chance of upward social mobility, and their need for work made them targets of resentment from white workers, and of exploitation by white owners.

A man who sought a change in this condition of helplessness was Philip Qipu Vundla. Born in Healdtown in the Eastern Cape in 1904, he was affectionately known as PQ.[11] In later life he moved to Johannesburg where he worked as a mine clerk. There he was active in the African Mine Workers' Union and organised protests against pass legislation and the forced removal of blacks from the Western Areas to Soweto in the mid-1950s. PQ was involved in many attempts to ameliorate the living conditions of his fellow blacks. He made representations for improved housing, education, working conditions and wages. He sought out government officials, formed several committees and associations and, wherever possible, provided help and comfort to those who came to him.

During the mid 1950s PQ became involved in the Moral Rearmament movement. This was to have a very definite Christian impact on his life and activities. His association with MRA caused him to meet whites who were sympathetic to the causes for which he was fighting. This was to become an important source of encouragement to him. In addition, MRA made it possible for him to travel in Europe and the USA, to address many meetings and to make contact with people outside South Africa.

PQ was active in such different organisations as the ANC (1952—1955) and the Soweto Urban Bantu Council (in 1968). Just before his death in 1969 he assisted in the establishment of ASSECA (Association for the Social, Educational and Cultural Advancement of the African People of SA). PQ:

> believed not only in changing men's minds but their hearts as well. He had a vision of a democratic and non-racial South Africa. He frequently said, 'I should care for the future of the white child as much as for the future of the black child'.[12]

Moreover, PQ was firmly committed to peaceful change and critical of violent solutions, believing that 'What you achieve through violence, you will need even greater violence to maintain,'[13] and 'that those who say blood-shed is the answer have other people's blood in mind, not their own.'[14]

The third area which involved the thought and activity of black Christian leaders was *education*. Chief Albert Luthuli, as a trained teacher of many years experience, was greatly concerned with the education of his fellow Africans. He was especially outspoken about the government's closure of many mission schools, the lack of adequate provision for African education and, most of all, about the system of Bantu Education introduced in 1955. He saw this as a scheme which would keep blacks in a condition of perpetual servanthood and ignorance:

> . . . the overall effect of this system (he said) is not educational at all but political. It is a tool in the hands of the white master for the more effective reduction and control of black servants.[15]

The fourth major issue is *political representation,* and here, too, black Christians have made their mark. Between 1910 and the 1960s blacks were to see their few political rights (the Cape franchise and the Coloured vote) slowly but surely eliminated and replaced with ineffectual boards of representatives. In 1927, the Hertzog bills proposed the removal of the Cape Native franchise which had supposedly been 'entrenched' in the Constitution of the Union. [16] In response:

> the ANC, under the presidency of the Rev ZR Mahabane from 1924, strongly attacked the bills in 1927, but refrained from protest activities or passive resistance. It relied on deputation, sought at the same time to build bridges with the Coloured and Indian movements, and participated in the conciliatory work of the Joint Councils of Europeans and Natives which had been established since 1921.[17]

It is noteworthy that despite the failure of petitions and representations, many black leaders retained confidence in the goodwill of whites and the establishment of a non-segregated structure in the not too distant future. There still existed in the 1920s a fair degree of optimism. DDT Jabavu, for example, wrote in 1928:

> It is our belief that with the spread of understanding in Church and college circles the future of South Africa is one we can contemplate with a fair degree of optimism in the hope that Christian influences will dispel illusions, transcend the mistaken political expedients of pseudo-segregationists and usher in a South Africa of racial peace and goodwill.[18]

However, as time went on, black leaders became more and more disinclined to listen to the promises of the government and the hopeful view of the liberals.

Following the victory of Malan's Nationalist Party in 1948, segregation and discrimination were strengthened, further legislated and strenuously enforced. In October 1948 twelve African leaders met in Bloemfontein to discuss their future policies. Xuma, Matthews and Jabavu were present, further evidence that in the 1950s Christians were amongst the political leaders of the African people.[19]. Along with lawyers, doctors, schoolteachers and businessmen, the elite of black professional and middle-class leadership always included ministers of religion.

It was in the Freedom Charter, adopted in Kliptown on the 25 and 26 June 1955 by the Congress of the People, that the convictions of many Africans — Christians included — were clearly stated; prefiguring subsequent Liberation Theology. The preamble reads:

> We, the People of South Africa, declare for all our country and the world to know: that South Africa belongs to all who live in it, black and white, and that no government can justly claim authority unless it is based on the will of all the people; that our people have been robbed of their birthright to land, liberty and peace by a form of government founded on injustice and inequality; that out country will never be prosperous or free until all our people live in brotherhood, enjoying equal rights and opportunities; that only a democratic state, based on the will of all the people, can secure to all their birthright without distinction of colour, race, sex or belief . . .[20]

Black Leaders and Christianity

Having dealt with the contribution of black Christian leaders to important socio-political and economic issues, we now turn to a brief discussion of their influence within the churches. In particular, significant themes in the thinking of two men will be mentioned, Chief Albert Luthuli and Bishop Alphaeus Zulu.

Luthuli was active in the Natal Missionary Conference as well as the Christian Council of South Africa. In 1948 he toured the USA as a guest of both the American Board and the North American Missionary Conference, and spoke in many places on Christian mission.

While he was committed to the propagation of the Christian faith in South Africa, he was critical of the type of Christianity that turned his people away from Christ:

> White paternalist Christianity — as though the whites have invented the Christian faith — estranged my people from Christ. Hypocrisy, double standards, and the identification of white skins with Christianity, do the same.[21]

He believed that the white churches should refrain from embarking on a patronising type of social service that was 'alien to the spirit of Christ'. This did not mean that the church should divorce itself from the affairs of its people. On the contrary, it should be involved with their lives and provide guidance and inspiration.[22]

Chief Luthuli was himself an example of this understanding of the task of the church. Throughout his life he sought to live out his Christian faith. It was for this reason that he could say of his activities in the ANC:

> For myself, I am in Congress precisely because I am a Christian. My Christian belief about human society must find expression here and now, and Congress is the spearhead of the real struggle. Some would have the communists excluded, others would have all non-communists withdraw from the Congress. My own urge because I am a Christian is to get into the thick of the struggle with other Christians, taking my Christianity with me and praying that it may be used to influence for good the character of the resistance.[23]

Meanwhile in the Africanist thinking of the PAC (Pan Africanist Congress), there was a fair measure of support for a particularly African Christianity. Thus, the African Independent Churches, because they were led by blacks and emphasised both African traditional religion and culture as valid and important, were regarded in a particularly favourable light by the PAC. Through these churches, the PAC had a firm link with the rural, peasant class as well as the urban Africans. It is significant that at the first PAC Convention (1959), Bishop Walter M Dimba, the Head of the Federation of Bantu Churches in South Africa, was asked to open the gathering with prayers and a sermon.[24]

If, instead of being banned in April 1960, the PAC had continued as a viable organisation, it may have succeeded in politicising the African Independent Churches, Nevertheless, it is important that it supported the idea of an African National Church, although some of its members later turned to Islam because of the injustices rationalised by the white churches.[25]

In 1971, Bishop Alphaeus Zulu (the first black man to be made an Anglican bishop in SA) was similarly calling for whites to make new laws and provide opportunities for the educational, social and economic advancement of black South Africans. On 17 May 1972, in delivering the TB Davie Memorial Lecture at the University of Cape Town, he argued that whites should acknowledge blacks as equal partners in the development of South Africa, as well as in the enjoyment of the fruits of that development. Nor did he fail to point out the significance of these urgent needs for Christianity. Amongst other things, he emphasised the extent to which Christianity had been compromised in the eyes of black people, and especially the black youth:

> If you are black and a Christian missionary how then do you respond to the black accusation that when the white men came to Africa, the black men had the land and the white men had the Bible, and now the black man has the Bible and white men the land?[26]

This question cannot, and must not, be avoided. If South Africa is to move beyond the present situation of anger, land hunger and, often, of poverty, it must be *satisfactorily* dealt with. Nor, however, is it possible for Black Theology to refuse to address itself to issues such as the usage of present black-owned and black-farmed land. In the homelands this question is particularly pertinent, for land ownership cannot be divorced from production and conservation. Perhaps it is time to move beyond the white accusation of inadequate black farming and the black defence of inadequate resources and over-population. Certainly, in terms of population as well as food and housing needs, co-operation, adaptation and change alone will make it possible to move towards a more secure future.

A secure future, however, cannot be achieved by the repression of those who are questioning the present structure of South African society. Nor can it be hoped for unless the views and feelings of the youth are taken into account. Therefore, Bishop Zulu's words regarding the views of young blacks need to be reiterated:

> Black youth charge more strongly than before, that the Christian religion is the opium which has made their parents tame and subservient; they are frustrated when whites of their own age groups engage in political activities with the government's blessing, especially when they are nationalists, while their own leaders have been banned or imprisoned, especially when they were nationalists.[27]

The path of survival for whites in South Africa, the Bishop said, lies not in discrimination and repression of blacks. For this will *not* ensure white preservation. The only possible future is for whites to adapt and adjust to a South Africa that is not based on white supremacy:

> Until now white South Africans have seen their hope for survival in a rigid exclusiveness of groups. They have regarded this as so extreme a priority that they have tolerated much that was grossly evil in human suffering to achieve it. The on-

ly possible crops, however, that will ever be reaped along this road are fear, suspicion, hatred and eventual mutual destruction.[28]

The people briefly discussed in the above paragraphs are, in terms of their emphasis on justice, freedom and racial equality, forerunners of modern Black Theology. Despite the many criticisms that can, and have, been levelled against them for elitism, naivete or ineffectiveness, they nevertheless represent an early form of black Christian resistance to white overlordship. The fact that they were less than successful in their resistance does not lessen their value and importance not least as a corrective to the view that South African Black Theology only began in the 1970s.

This brings us to the end of this introductory analysis of the opinions and concerns that dominated the first six decades of black Christian thought in this century. In this period, at least three themes arose which will be the subject of the successive chapters of this book. The first is the desire on the part of blacks *to live out the Gospel as Africans* rather than as Europeans. This theme is particularly clearly expressed in the activities of the African Independent Churches, and to a lesser extent, in the Africanist ideas of the PAC. The second theme is *black identity*, the view that blacks should seek not to deny their own identity, that they should refuse to be patronised and looked down upon, that they should be conscious of their uniqueness and live it out in terms of their Christian conviction. Thirdly, there is the desire for *liberation from exploitation* and freedom to live, and act, as full partners in South African society and the Church.

However, before embarking upon an analysis of African Theology (Chapters 3 and 4), Black Consciousness (Chapter 5) and Black Liberation (Chapter 6), some time must be spent in seeking to place South African Black Theology in an international theological context. This will be my task in Chapter 2.

Notes

1 See for example, P Hinchliff, *The Church in South Africa* (London: SPCK, 1968), F Wilson and D Perrot (eds), *Outlook on a Century* (Lovedale Press, Lovedale, and Spro-Cas, 1972) and J W de Gruchy, *The Church Struggle in South Africa* (Grand Rapids: Eerdmans, 1979, and Cape Town: David Philip, 1979).

2 de Gruchy, *ibid*, p13.

3 Quoted in *ibid* p8. For further discussion see A Boesak, 'Is Apartheid Kerke se skuld?' *Pro Veritate* (February, 1973) pp5—7 and 21—23.

4 de Gruchy, *ibid*, p48. For a comprehensive record of African leadership see Thomas Karis and Gwendolyn M Carter (eds), *From Protest to Challenge: A Documentary History of African Politics in South Africa 1882—1964*, Volumes 1—4 (Stanford, California: Hoover Institution Press, 1972) and Gail Gerhart,

Black Power in South Africa: The Evolution of an Ideology (Los Angeles and London: Univ of California Press, 1978).

5 See Karis and Carter, *ibid,* (Vol 4), pp39—43, 79—81 and 60—63.

6 Founded in 1912, and variously called the South African Native National Congress, African Native Congress and Native Congress. Later it became the African National Congress. Cf Matthew's autobiography *Freedom for my People* (Cane Town: David Philip, 1983).

7 A Luthuli, *Let My People Go* (Glasgow: Collins/Fontana 1962/3), p39.

8 See T Dunbar Moodie, *The Rise of Afrikanerdom: Power, Apartheid and Afrikaner Civil Religion* (London: Univ of California Press, 1975) and WA de Klerk, *The Puritans in Africa: A Story of Afrikanerdom* (Harmondsworth, Middlesex: Penguin, 1975).

9 TRH Davenport, *South Africa: A Modern History* (Johannesburg: Macmillan, 1977), p331ff.

10 de Gruchy, *op cit,* p37.

11 See a biography by his wife K Vundla, *PQ: The Story of Philip Vundla of South Africa* (Johannesburg: Moral Rearmament, 1973). She gives his birth date as 1904. See also Karis and Carter, *From Protest to Challenge* Vol 4, p163, who give it as 1901.

12 K Vundla, *PQ: The Story of Philip Vundla of South Africa,* p74.

13 *Ibid.*

14 *Ibid,* p94.

15 A Luthuli, *op cit,* p45.

16 In 1936 Africans (those few who had 'qualified' for the franchise) were removed from the common voters roll and placed on a separate roll. They were to be represented in Parliament, Senate and on the Provincial Councils by whites, and had to be content with what later became the Native Representative Councils. By 1951 the latter were abolished by the Nationalists and by 1959 the white representatives in the central government were replaced, with a promise of eventual homeland independence. (See Davenport *op cit,* p333)

17 TRH Davenport, *op cit,* p212.

18 DDT Jabavu, *The Segregationist Fallacy and Other Papers* (Alice, 1928), p24. Quoted in G Gerhart, *Black Power in South Africa,* p35.

19 Gail Gerhart, *op cit,* pp137—145.

20 A Luthuli, *op cit,* p212ff, discusses these and related events.

21 *Ibid,* p119.

22 *Ibid,* pp118 and 124.

23 *Ibid,* p138.

24 See G Gerhart, *op cit,* p202 and B Sundkler, *Bantu Prophets in South Africa,*(Oxford: Oxford Univ Press, 1948/1961) pp306—307.

25 G Gerhart, *ibid,* pp202—204.

26 A Zulu, *The Dilemma of the Black South African,* (Univ of Cape Town, 1972) p5.

27 *Ibid,* p10.

28 *Ibid,* p13.

CHAPTER TWO

The Broader Theological Context

As was shown in chapter one, black Christians had already spoken out on many issues early on in the 20th century. These included socio-economic discrimination, lack of political representation and pseudo-Christianity. However, the rise of specifically African, Black and Liberation Theologies only occurred during the 1960s and 70s.[1] But before surveying and analysing these in the South African context, the broader theological context must be briefly dealt with. This is because South African Black Theology is certainly related to, and influenced by these theologies, to a greater or lesser extent. Many of the issues that will be dealt with in the later chapters will simply be raised here, and the relationship between South African Black Theology and other theologies briefly mentioned.

African Theology

Many people believe that Christianity first came to Africa as a result of the preaching of the 19th century missionaries. In fact, this is not so. Early in the church's history Christianity flourished in North Africa and also in what is today called Ethiopia. John S Pobee (Professor of New Testament at the University of Ghana, Legon) has written:

> Christianity, originating in Palestine, came to Africa by a circuitous route. Of course, Christianity appeared in Egypt and Roman North Africa, not to mention Nubia, in the first three centuries of the church's existence, long before Western Europe was Christianised.[2]

Not only was Christianity to be found in these areas, but it also produced influential churchmen like Augustine and Tertullian:

> North African Christianity not only produced theological giants like Augustine of

Hippo, Tertullian and Cyprian, but also left indelible marks on Latin Christianity. Indeed a good deal of what became Latin Christianity, or Christianity of the West, bears the marks of Augustine and Tertullian.[3]

The Ethiopian Church was also African. The Coptic faith may well date back to the Ethiopian eunuch of Acts 8. 26—40 but, whatever its origins, it was flourishing long before the 19th century.[4]

There was also limited contact with the Portuguese explorers and traders, especially along the West coast of Africa, to which several stone crosses still bear testimony. Finally, and of special significance for South Africa, there was of course the Dutch settlement at the Cape in the 17th century. This was the thin edge of the wedge, with all that this was to signify, of European penetration into the southern tip of the African continent.

These earlier manifestations were limited geographically and, in North Africa, almost completely overshadowed by the advance of Islam in the 8th century. It was, therefore, only as a result of the efforts of 19th century missionaries that the African Church, as it is known today, came into being. A great deal has been written about the missionaries and their work and I do not propose here to enter into a discussion of their merits or demerits. It is however, indisputable that African Theology, in the broadest sense of an African understanding and expression of Christianity, could not have come about if the Gospel had not been preached to Africans by these missionaries.

At this point it is necessary to distinguish between 'popular' and 'academic' theology. Popular theology grows directly out of the life of the Church in its response to the Gospel, eg sermons, hymns, prayers, rituals, etc. Academic theology is usually more concerned with a systematic study of concepts of God, the interpretation of beliefs and customs and an analysis of the relation between Christianity and African traditional religion. In this book, I will be unable fully to describe or discuss African church life, but will concentrate on the theological writings of black theologians and churchmen.

The more scholarly African Theology was slow to take form, the most important reason probably being that leadership in the churches and theological seminaries was largely in the hands of white men. As these people determined both the concerns and content of study and generally had a low opinion of African culture and tradition, a distinctively African Theology was not really propagated. This situation began to change only in this century and by the end of World War Two, the African church was very different to what it had been in the 1850s.

Several factors contributed to this change: the numerical growth and importance of the Churches, the competence (and frustration) of its leaders and the broader context of African nationalism and independence from direct colonial rule. More Africans began to occupy positions of leadership in schools, theological colleges and universities. Out of their reflection, as *African* Christians, African theology began to take shape.

By the late 1960s, the 'first flowerings' of African Theology had begun to appear in the writings of Harry Sawyerr (Sierra Leone), E Bolaji Idowu (Nigeria), John Mbiti (Kenya) and Kwesi Dickson (Ghana). Several Christian conferences were held (Ibadan in 1958 and 1965, Kampala in 1963 and Abidjan in 1969), where interest in African Theology was expressed and developed.

African Theology, then, should be seen in the light of a determination to redress the previous neglect of relating the Gospel to the broad range of African thought, tradition and experience. Since the 1960s, African Theology has been explored and expanded — by both Africans and Europeans — and not least in Southern Africa. It is only to be expected that many of the concerns of African Theology will be of great interest to the African population of South Africa. In chapters three and four, the nature and the implications of the Africanisation of Christianity will be examined.

Black Theology in the USA

South African Black Theology also bears a close relationship to Black Theology in the USA. This does not mean that the two are exactly the same, nor that black theologians in South Africa are entirely dependent on the ideas of their counterparts in the USA. But there are several common themes and black South African theologians such as Allan Boesak have been influenced by American theologians like James Cone, Professor at Union Theological Seminary in New York.

Black Theology in the USA has its roots in the black slave churches which were formed in the 16th century. Although these churches were initially subservient to and dependent upon the white churches, they provided an essential spiritual foundation for the development of Black Theology in the 20th century. In these churches the dilemma of blacks was first seen in a theological context, and the search for freedom and identity, for humanity and opportunity, was associated with God's promises in the Bible. It was also in the black churches, and amongst such groups as the Quakers, that the battle against slavery and its so-called theological justification was begun. It was, in effect, these same struggles and hopes, albeit in the 20th century context, that were at the base of the civil rights movement and later of Black Theology.[5]

During the 1950s and 60s, American blacks, or negroes as they were then called, were increasingly critical of their experience and status in American society. The theological nature of this reflection and criticism was most clearly expressed in the strong church base of Martin Luther King's civil rights struggles. Although King was not the only influential figure in this period, he typifies the *theological* basis of the black discontent with the discrimination practised against them in the USA.[6]

However, not all were in agreement with King's views and policies, and even before his assassination, the civil rights movement had gained momentum and was increasingly radicalised by the advocates of Black Power such as Stokely Carmichael and James Baldwin. By the late 60s and early 70s, a deliberately formulated Black Theology had begun to take shape.

On 26 April 1969, the Black Manifesto was issued. The signatories denounced the American government as racist and imperialist, called for the liberation of all people in the USA, rejected capitalism and demanded reparations to the tune of 500 million dollars. Moreover, it strongly criticised both the white church and Jewish synagogues as racist in the extreme.[7]

Together with subsequent pronouncements by the National Conference of Black Churchmen (NCBC), the Black Manifesto was a clear indication of the growing radicalisation of black leaders (both Christian and non-Christian) and their estrangement from the white churches.[8] Thus, by the start of the 1970s, some black churchmen had become much more critical, demanding and aggressive than Martin Luther King had been. With the publication of James Cone's *Black Theology and Black Power* in 1969, Black Theology began to take on a distinctive and definite form.[9]

The major emphases of North American Black Theology have been on black consciousness, liberation from white domination and racism, black self-determination and black power. The church, and society in general, have come under the critical scrutiny of black theologians, who have also adopted a situationalist emphasis, stressing that the life situation of blacks should be the starting point of theological thinking, and should be regarded as of prime importance in the way in which the Bible is read and interpreted. Otherwise, theology would become irrelevant and merely be a means of control exercised by the white community.

Although James Cone is the major figure in the Black Theology of the USA, he is certainly not its only representative. Others, like Gayraud S Wilmore and J Deotis Roberts, have also made their contributions. Roberts, especially, would seem closer in tone and content to the majority of South African black theologians than some of his compatriots. This can be illustrated by his views on reconciliation:

> Reconciliation can only take place when blacks as well as whites are free to affirm their authentic selfhood and peoplehood. There can be no Christian reconciliation between oppressors and the oppressed. We are called to Christian maturity in the body of Christ. The new humanity in the fellowship of believers requires that all

God's children be *free and equal* . . . The only Christian way in race relations is a liberating experience of reconciliation for the white oppressor as well as for the black oppressed. This is what Black political Theology is all about, and its message is to the whole church of Christ.[10]

The implications of Black Theology for South Africa will be discussed in chapter five.

It is thus a mistake to regard theologians like Cone as necessarily representative of the black church as a whole. In fact, many black US churches do not fully espouse the views of the country's black theologians, although, as in South Africa, the actual facts and figures are not available. More research, in the sense of field work amongst congregations, has to be done, in order to assess the extent of the influence of Black Theology on the churches as well as on the black population as a whole. This is because, although Cone, or Boesak and others, are regarded as spokesmen, the extent to which their views are actually representative still needs to be accurately established. Only then will we be able more fully to assess the impact of their thinking.

What, then, is the relationship between Black Theology in the USA and the African Theology of the African continent? From the outset, black theologians in the USA consistently sought to affirm their solidarity with Africa. In 1972 James Cone, for example, argued that the common experience of suffering as a result of their blackness, and the common hope of liberation, were vitally important factors which resulted in Black and African Theology being drawn together.[11] But African theologians such as J Mbiti have not always responded to this overture because of what they regarded as the differing needs and interests of the North American and African situations. In 1974 Mbiti wrote:

Black Theology cannot and will not become African Theology. Black Theology and African Theology emerge from quite different historical and contemporary situations . . . Black Theology hardly knows the situation of Christians living in Africa, and therefore its direct relevance for Africa is non-existent or only accidental.[12]

Mbiti did, however, say that whilst Black Theology was not in his opinion relevant to independent Africa, it was relevant to the South African situation.

This was not to be the final word on the subject. Mbiti's view was subsequently questioned in two ways. Firstly, by South African Black Theology and, secondly, by a call for Black Liberation within Africa.

The initial criticism from a South African black theologian was voiced by Bishop Desmond Tutu, who pointed out that in South Africa the concerns of African, Black and Liberation Theology come together.[13]

The other criticism came from a younger group of African theologians. For example, at the Pan-African Conference of Third World Theologians held in Accra, Ghana, in December 1977, both Black and African Theologians were speaking of the liberation of the black masses.[14] For, although it was true that in terms of culture and African traditional religion Mbiti was largely correct, the problems of elitism in post-independent black rule in Africa as well as the feeling of political powerlessness of blacks in the United States, issued in a combined call for the liberation of the black masses. This theme will be taken up in chapters five and six.

This emphasis on liberation brings us to the question: What is Liberation Theology?

Latin American Liberation Theology

Christianity was first introduced to the people of Central and Latin America by the Portuguese and Spanish in the 16th century. As a result of the close relationship between Church and State in the Iberian Peninsula at that time, the conquest and colonisation of the indigenous population took place with the compliance, and even assistance, of the Church. As time went on and greater numbers of settlers, officials and priests came to Latin America, the Catholic Church became increasingly associated, indeed integrated, with the structures of power and privilege. Although it has been shown that certain individuals attempted to improve the living conditions and opportunities of the indigenous people, the Church, as an institution, did little along these lines.[15]

It has only been during this century that this situation has begun to change. During the last four decades, there has been a marked change in the understanding of Protestants and Catholics of the role of the Church in the socio-political and economic realities of the Latin American continent.

During the 1950s several development programmes came into being, centred on the effort of the poorer countries in the world to progress to the position of the richer countries. In many cases, the technological structures and cultural modes of the Western countries were uncritically accepted as goals. Whereas the 1950s were characterised by hope, by the 1960s disillusionment had set in. Many in the third world became critical of 'developmentism', for several reasons: they asked whether the life-styles of other countries were necessarily desirable, whether the 'first world' was not simply perpetuating the poverty of the 'third world' for its own benefit and whether development, in the final analysis, amounted to anything more than cosmetic change. The beginnings of Liberation Theology were marked by a transition from the development programmes of the 1950s and by the consistent concern to see structural changes in Latin American societies. In pursuit of these changes,

Liberation Theology moved towards its contemporary alignment with Marxist analysis and socialist politics.[16]

As early as 1962, the ISAL movement (Church and Society in Latin America) was started under the auspices of the World Council of Churches. Then, in 1974, Ruben Alves published an article in the ISAL magazine, *Christiano v Sociedad*, in which he outlined the six main points of what was later to become Liberation Theology. These were: 1) the underdevelopment of the Third World is a result of the exploitation of the developed countries; 2) the class struggle is the dominant feature of life in Latin America; 3) the essence of Christianity is the humanisation of society; 4) God is working directly in the world and not just in and through the Church; 5) the work of God is evident in revolutionary movements which the Church must, therefore, become a part of; and 6) Marx is a symbol of the hidden essence of Christianity and thus Christians must unite with Marxists in the task of humanisation.[17] In chapter six, I hope to show that some, but certainly not all of these, occur in Black Liberation Theology in South Africa.

The acceptance of a political theology by Catholic priests was made evident in a letter addressed to the Third World by eighteen bishops in 1967 and at a Conference held in Medellin, Colombia, in 1968.[18]

At least two major themes arose at Medellin. On the one hand, the Catholic bishops addressed the various socio-economic situations in their countries, and, on the other, they addressed themselves to the Church. In no uncertain terms, they criticised the vast gap between the rich and the poor; the international system of economic dependency practised by 'first world' countries against 'third world' countries; and the 'institutionalised violence' practised by several of their governments. They denounced low wages, harsh working conditions, unemployment, poverty and discrimination, in short, the exploitation of the poor and powerless. In the strongest possible terms they appealed for a new and more just social order to be instituted, in which more than a few powerful individuals could participate.

The second central emphasis at Medellin was the need for 'new forms of the Church's presence' in Latin America. Catholic leaders were opposed to the Church continuing to act as a legitimising authority for the status quo. They believed that it should not side with the rich and the powerful against the poor and powerless. It was for this reason that they spoke of the need for the church to exercise its prophetic role and, like the prophets of the Old Testament, to speak out against injustice, cruelty and greed, or, in modern parlance, exploitation.

Some within the Latin American Church, and especially individuals such as Paulo Freire, emphasised the need for a conscientising evangelism which did not simply concentrate on a person's soul or spiritual condition but made people more aware of their situation in *this* world and encouraged the oppressed to fight against the injustices perpetuated against them. Individual spiritual and moral change alone simply played into the hands of the oppressors unless it also initiated radical (structural) social change. Finally, it was recommended that the Church review its own structure and ministry, adopt a lifestyle of service rather than luxury, and carry out its mission 'in poverty and under oppression'.[19]

In going about this task, Liberation Theology has placed a great deal of emphasis on hermeneutics (interpretation) and especially on Biblical hermenuetics. As this issue is more fully discussed in chapter six, only a few brief comments are necessary here. In essence, liberation hermeneutics regards the Exodus narrative in the Old Testament and Luke 4.18—19 in the New Testament as *the* key passages in the Bible. In the Lukan passage, Jesus reads this section from the book of Isaiah:

> The spirit of the Lord is upon me because he has appointed me to preach the Gospel to the poor. He has sent me to proclaim release to the captives, and recovery of sight to the blind, to set free those who are down-trodden, to proclaim the favourable year of the Lord.

The basic theme of God's purpose is thus identified as liberation, a liberation that is radical and extensive, that is both individual and social, spiritual and political, moral as well as structural.

Since the Medellin Conference, numerous books and articles developing these and other themes have been published by theologians like R Alves, J Miguez-Bonino, Gustavo Gutierrez, Hugo Assman, Leonardo Boff, Juan Luis Segundo and S Croatto, to mention but a few. Liberation Theology is today an ever-growing and diverse movement, and is having a profound impact on many people all over the world.[20]

Against this sketch of the concerns and development of Latin American Liberation Theology, the question must be asked: How does this affect South African Black Theology?

In 1979, Dr Adrian Hastings wrote of African Theology:

> It is not, all in all, surprising that 'African Theology' would come to be challenged, but also balanced, by a 'Black Theology', based in Southern Africa and much more influenced by Afro-American Black Theology and Latin American 'Liberation Theology'.[21]

As I will indicate in the following chapters, it would seem that, however influential the Latin American Liberation theologians have recently become, South African Black Theology, in its origins, was scarcely affected by them at all. In fact, the liberationist theme came to the fore more as a result of Cone's writings, than of the Latin Americans. It is only recently that a direct Latin

American influence has become more apparent. However, as I will seek to show, while Black Theology in South Africa uniquely incorporates elements of the African, Black and Liberation Theologies, the rise of South African Black Theology can be explained *less* by a theory of subversive external influences *than by* a dynamic interplay between the South African situation itself, and the creative application of both local and external insights to it.

Notes

1 Black Theology and Liberation Theology, it must be remembered, are part of, and also an extension of, the political theology of Europe in the 1960s. As a result of the work of German scholars like Johannes Baptist Metz, and later, Jurgen Moltmann, a new trend developed in theology. This 'political theology' was an attempt to theologise concerning human nature and the goals of society. Theology was related to the principles of social order and development so that the church could be effectively involved in social change rather than simply succumbing to social apathy. Related to, and following from, these theological trends were the increasing politicisation of the World Council of Churches (WCC), debates on church and society at Vatican II (1962—65), the dialogue between Christianity and Marxism and the Theology of Revolution. Many of the subsequent 'political' theologies of the third world were definitely influenced by the above thinkers and theological movements. Cf J Moltmann, JB Metz *et al* (eds), *Religion and Political Society* (New York: Harper and Row, 1974) and A Kee (ed) *A Reader in Political Theology* (London: SCM, 1974).

2 John S Pobee, *Towards an African Theology* (Nashville: Abingdon, 1979) p15.

3 *Ibid.* See also Byang H Kato, 'Christianity as an African Religion' *Ev RT* 4:1 (1980) pp33—36 (reprinted from *Perception*, May 1979), and Ieuan P Ellis, 'In Defence of North African Christianity' in Mark E Glasswell and EW Fasholé-Luke (eds), *New Testament Christianity for Africa and the World* (London: SPCK, 1974) pp157—165.

4 See John Mbiti, 'The Future of Christianity in Africa (1970—2000)' *Com Via* 13 (1970) pp19—38.

5 See GS Wilmore and JH Cone (eds), *Black Theology: A Documentary History , 1966—1979* (New York: Orbis, 1979) pp120f and 154—162.

6 See Martin Luther King, *Strength to Love* (London: Fontana/Collins, 1963); *Chaos or Commmunity* (Harmondsworth: Penguin, 1969); Coretta Scott King, *My Life with Martin Luther King Jr* (London: Hodder and Stoughton, 1969) and Gayraud S Wilmore and James H Cone (eds), *Black Theology: A Documentary History 1966—1979* pp1—64.

7 Wilmore and Cone, (eds) *ibid*, pp80—89.

8 This process has been documented in *ibid,* in a chapter entitled 'The Attack on White Religion' pp67—132.

9 *Black Theology and Black Power* (New York: Seabury Press, 1969).

10 J Deotis Roberts, *A Black Political Theology* (Philadelphia: Westminster Press, 1974) p222. For a brief discussion of Black Evangelicals in the USA see Ronald C Potter, 'The New Black Evangelicals' in GS Wilmore and JH Cone (eds), *op cit* pp302—309.

11 See Wilmore and Cone (eds), *ibid,* pp463—476 as well as pp80—81 and 249.

12 J Mbiti, 'An African views American Black Theology' in Wilmore and Cone (eds), *ibid,* p481.

13 D Tutu, 'Black Theology/African Theology — Soul Mates or Antagonists?' in Wilmore and Cone (eds) *ibid,* p490.

14 See Kofi Appiah-Kubi and Sergio Torres (eds), *African Theology en Route* (Maryknoll, New York: Orbis Books, 1979) pp67, 155ff, 189ff, Wilmore and Cone (eds), *ibid,* pp495—601 and H Haselbarth, 'The Relevance of Black Theology for Independent Africa' (paper read at Jos, Nigeria in September, 1975) pp1—19.

15 P Perez, 'Liberationistic Roots in Latin America', *Theological Fraternity Bulletin* 3 (1974) pp9—12.

16 See A Kee, *A Reader in Political Theology,* (London: SCM, 1974) pp66—95.

17 Unpublished paper by R Hundley, 'Introduction to Latin American Liberation Theology', (presented to the Theological Society, St John's College, Cambridge, 3 November, 1981) p2. For a further discussion of ISAL see Emilio A Nuñez, 'The Theology of Liberation in Latin America' *Ev RT* 3:1 (1979) pp37—51.

18 From the outset, Latin American Liberation Theology was enormously influenced by European political theology. Besides Moltmann and Metz, thinkers such as Dietrich Bonhoeffer, Richard Shaull, Paul Lehmann, Harvey Cox and of course Karl Marx have also contributed to the development of what today is broadly termed 'Latin American Liberation Theology.'

19 See Gustavo Gutierrez, *A Theology of Liberation* (London: SCM, 1974) pp101—119.

20 For a good introduction to some of these see (ed) Rosino Gibellini, *Frontiers of Theology in Latin America* (London: SCM, 1974). See also Francis P Fiorenza, 'Latin American Liberation Theology', *Interpretation* 28 (1974) pp441—457.

21 A Hastings, *A History of Christianity in Africa: 1950—1975* (Cambridge: University Press, 1979) p232.

CHAPTER THREE

The Africanisation of Christianity

Africanisation, as the term is used in this chapter, essentially means 'indigenisation', or better still 'contextualisation', the process by which Christianity is accepted into African patterns of thought and behaviour. Having been accepted, as it were, into the heart of Africa, the Gospel must, like leaven, work itself through the entire structure, changing, adapting and using all that it finds there. Obviously, this process does not take place on its own. People need to study, experiment and come to an understanding of how entire societies can become Christianised. Not simply to engineer the establishment of a superficial and external religion, but rather, the true conversion and transformation of individuals, churches and communities. A task that *African Christians*, especially, are most suited to carry out.

African Theology, then, is quite simply Christian Theology written in the context of Africa, bearing in mind the needs of Africa and the Gospel's message to Africa. A South African, Z Kurewa, has defined African Theology as:

> The study that seeks to reflect upon and express the Christian faith in African thought forms and idioms as it is experienced in African Christian communities and always in dialogue with the rest of Christendom.[1]

This does not mean that Africans are cutting themselves off from the rest of the world, nor indeed writing an exclusive theology. Rather, it means that there is a vision fully to understand and live the Gospel as Africans, rather than as Americans or Europeans. In fact, amongst some, there is even the vision of a great African Church making its contribution towards the international church in terms of theology, mission and church life.

For those who wonder about the validity of such an enterprise, African Theologians have not been slow to point out that the attempt to understand Christianity from a particular perspective, for the express purpose of making it relevant and meaningful to those to whom it is addressed, has been in process throughout the many centuries of Church history. From the early to the modern church, theologians have been engaged in the task of intepreting and presenting the Christian faith to the people of their time. African Theology in this century and on this continent is engaged in this very task, that of the intelligible proclamation of the Gospel.

'African Theology' encompasses a broad spectrum of thought. There can be no single African Theology, for it is the theological response of thousands of different African peoples within varying ecclesiastical traditions (Protestant, Catholic or Independent).[2] Despite this qualification, however, it remains valid to speak of African Theology as representing a large group of Christians who have several beliefs and experiences in common.

An important common area is that of the response, indeed criticism, by Africans to what they call 'the white man's religion'. This does not refer to the Christian faith *per se* but to this plus Western culture, world views and prejudices. It is to these additional factors and attitudes that African Theology strongly objects.[3]

African Theology has deliberately addressed itself to the question of Christianity's contribution to, and relevance in, an African context. The need for this task has been indicated by Bishop Desmond Tutu:

> Until fairly recently, the African Christian has suffered from a form of religious schizophrenia. With a part of himself he has been compelled to pay lip service to Christianity as understood, expressed and preached by the white man. But with an even greater part of himself, a part he has been often ashamed to acknowledge openly, and which he has struggled to repress, he has felt that his Africanness was being violated . . . [moreover] he was being redeemed from sins he did not believe he had committed; he was being given answers, and often splendid answers, to questions he had not asked.[4]

It was for this reason that the Gospel, as it was preached in the 'mission churches', was, in some of its emphases, irrelevant to the experience and questions of Africans. As a result, Christianity was not able to touch, renew or become part of the inner core of the experience of African believers.

African Theology objects to the fact that Christianity (when interpreted in a purely Western sense) has been used to deny the value of African identity, culture and world-views. Thus, instead of the Christian faith working as leaven within African society, converts often tended to live in an uneasy balance between African and Western world views.

African theologians have not simply placed the blame on white shoulders. For, although they have censured them for the 'Westernness' of the Church, both in the past and in the present, their own failure has also been acknowledged.

> We African Theologians are quite as much to blame as anyone else, for we find it much easier to regurgitate what was fed into us, than to use our acquired skills for creative theological thinking.[5]

This emphasis on the development of an African Christianity must, however, not be seen to be a mere harking back to the past. African theologians do not want simply to return to the old way of life, but rather, in the context of the Christian faith, to preserve that which is valuable in traditional African life and religion, to respond to the challenge of contemporary African experience.

Bishop Manas Buthelezi has distinguished between what he terms an 'ethnographic approach' and an 'anthropological approach',[6] rejecting the former because it tends to treat the African world-view(s) as an isolated, independent entity and may also lead to a romanticisation of the past. The 'anthropological approach', on the other hand, rather than seeking to live in the past, relates to the present-day concerns of black people, whether these be cultural, political or whatever. It preserves that which is valuable and useful to Africans in a modern context, recognising that the old days are gone and that Africans must adapt and contribute to both the present and the future.

The overriding concern of African Theology is thus its emphasis on a *holistic salvation*, not salvation that affects only the 'soul' or 'spiritual things' but one that touches, heals and changes all of life. This follows from an African world-view which is predominantly ontological, ie that religion is the essence of life. It is not a separate, spiritual compartment, but an attitude that penetrates life as a whole. It may well be that such a model is closer to the biblical view than that of a primary Western (Greek) separation of the material and the spiritual.

In the attempt to articulate what this implies for African Christianity, several themes have received attention: the meaning and value of African traditional religion, African ancestors, African culture and socio-political issues. An examination of these will be the task of this chapter. Then, in chapter four, the African Independent Churches will be discussed to further examine and illustrate the Africanisation of Christianity.

Christianity and African Traditional Religion

Early in the 19th century John Campbell wrote this concerning the black tribes of South Africa:

> . . . they have scarcely any religion: but some of them profess to believe that some great being came from above, and made the world after which he returned and cared no more about it. It is very probable that even this feeble ray of light was ob-

tained by means of their intercourse with the Dutch Boers during several ages.[7]

It is views such as these that African theologians have sought to counteract, by showing that the worshippers of traditional African religions were not completely ignorant of God. In other words, they are challenging the assertion that Africans came to know God only once the Christian gospel had been preached to them.[8]

This is in agreement with the view expressed at the Consultation of African Theologians in Ibadan (Nigeria) in 1965, ie that the African knowledge of God through Christ 'is not totally discontinuous with our peoples' previous knowledge of him.'[9] This is borne out in a statement by a black South African, IK Shuuya, who said at the Consultation of the Missiological Institute in Mapumulo (Natal) in 1972:

> . . . for every society in Africa one thing was evident, namely that someone exists above all. He has the power and is almighty. The African societies witness to this idea by coining several names for the Supreme Being (Gods).[10]

If what Shuuya (and others) have said is true, Africans cannot be said to be either incapable of metaphysical thought or devoid of religious faith. On the contrary, awareness of God and to a lesser extent direct worship of God was an important feature of African life prior to the work of Christian evangelisation.

The meeting point between the African peoples' 'previous knowledge of Him' and their knowledge of God through Christ needs to be analysed in greater depth. Shuuya does not discuss the extent of African knowledge of God nor the source of that knowledge, ie was it as a result of 'natural revelation', or the direct operation of the Holy Spirit, or even a memory of God from the origin of human history?[11]

Although African theologians are agreed that there is some continuity between traditional African and Christian concepts of God, there are various opinions as to the extent of this continuity.

On the one hand, there are those who assert that the relationship between traditional and biblical belief is, in fact, one of direct continuity. SP Legida, for example, does not distinguish between conceptions of Yahweh, Nkulunkulu, Modimo, Badimo, Thixo, and Qamata.[12] A better-known author, GM Setiloane, in his vehement criticism of 'the Western Christian image of God', goes as far as to assert the superiority of the traditional African gods:

> Put tauntingly, it [African Theology] says that the Western Christian theologians' 'God' could easily die because he is so small and human. The Sotho-Tswana God, according to me, the Ngo people's God, according to Gaba, and the Kikuyu

peoples' God, according to Kibicho, could never die because it has no human limitations and is so immense, incomprehensible, wide, tremendous and unique.[13]

Not only is Setiloane critical of the Western Christian theologians' God — a very broad category at best — but he also questions the supremacy and finality of the revelation of Jesus Christ:

> We are not necessarily agreed as to the supremacy, and the right to supercede all else, of the revelation of the Man of Nazareth. Kibicho very strongly disputes this right over the revelation of this same Divinity to our fathers.[14]

Setiloane here, and elsewhere, is reacting primarily to the outright rejection of the traditional gods by Christian missionaries. At times, the strength of this reaction leads almost to a rejection of the biblical God or, at least, to a tendency to see the African and the Christian God as being on one and the same level. Whereas true empathy is a necessary response to the first tendency, I feel that the second is another matter altogether. There can be no straight transition from Yahweh or Christ to Thixo or Nkulunkulu. Not only because of the Christian emphasis on special revelation, but also because of several clear differences between people's conceptions and experience of these various 'Supreme Gods'.

On the other hand, not all African theologians would agree with the approach adopted by Legida and Setiloane.[15] Thus, Simon Gqubule has emphasised that in Christ we have the final revelation, and he affirms the supremacy and authority of the Christian revelation of God in Christ.[16] Further, in response to those African theologians who have advocated a return to the traditional religions or have sought to emphasise the importance of the ancestors (either as objects of worship or as intemediaries with God) he says:

> For the Christian only the Triune God can be the object of worship; moreover the Christian scriptures say: 'There is *one God*, and also *one mediator* between God and man, Christ Jesus (1 Tim. 2:5).'[17]

The importance of this emphasis on the authority of the Bible has been spelt out by the white theologian David Bosch,[18] who believes that African religion cannot be visualised as a pyramid structure, with God at the apex, followed in decreasing order by the ancestors, man, the animals and lifeless objects. He argues that the African religious structure should be visualised as a globe rather than as a pyramid. The globe consists of the religious life and experience of the community, with the belief in God as the base upon which the globe rests. He adds that the biblical God cannot simply be *added* to such a framework of understanding nor can He simply replace the role of a traditional god, for misconceptions about God's nature will inevitably result. Religion is not a separate facet, but closely interrelated with many other conceptions and practices within African life.

For this reason Bosch speaks of the need for continuity and discontinuity with respect to belief in God,[19] continuity, in that there are similarities in African and Christian conceptions of God, such as the recognition of God's transcendence and power, which provide a meaningful and valid point of reference. Discontinuity is also necessary, ie the rejection of conceptions which conflict with the biblical view, such as the common African view of God as a *deus absconditus* (absent God), a God whose transcendence and distance remove him from the affairs of life, leaving mediators such as the ancestors very much in control, and causing people seeking to approach him directly only in situations of dire emergency.

If this need for both continuity and discontinuity is recognised and put into effect, the result will be that African concepts of God will be both transformed and effectively incorporated, depending on their value and truth. In fact, African religion will thus be subject to the same purification and renewal that was the case in the many years of mission to the tribes and nations of Europe. In the same way as the Greek/Roman gods such as Zeus and Jupiter were superceded, so were the 'European' Wodan and Freya. It must not be forgotten that the Christian Church often destroyed, undermined or adapted pagan festivals and places of worship for its own purposes. This process is necessary, perhaps inevitable, but nevertheless fraught with difficulties, because the Christian Gospel must seek to retain its authority and uniqueness without callously demolishing other religious notions, or needlessly alienating those to whom it is addressed.

This discussion of God in African Theology cannot end without reference being made to the worship of God. African Theology (especially at the church level) is concerned not so much with the clarification of a 'concept' of God, as with a vibrant response of praise and thanksgiving in the worship of God by believers. M Mabona rightly asks:

> Why are forms of Christian worship so stilted and restrained? . .. Why the awkward gap between people and ministers? . . . Let there be no participators and spectators in our worship. We are all participators in God's bounty and spectators of his works of loving kindness.[20]

In this context the forms of worship in dance, song and prayer have been mentioned. Adrian Hastings has drawn attention to the signficance of the musical revolution that accompanied the Catholic programme of liturgical revision in Africa:

It had increasingly been realised that the failure of the churches to make use of African tunes and song forms and the imposition of narrowly translated western hymns with their tunes theoretically unchanged was a grave source of weakness in popular worship, while the strength of the independent churches often lay in their music.[21]

Tutu has taken the issue further by asking:

Why should we feel that something is amiss if our theology is too dramatic for verbalisation but can be expressed only adequately in the joyous song and the scintillating movement of Africa's dance in the liturgy?[22]

Although these important themes have not been dealt with extensively by black South African theologians, there can be no doubt that on a more 'popular' level, liturgical revisions and initiatives are by no means foreign to the experience of African church-goers both in the 'mission' and 'independent' church contexts.

Christian Faith and African Ancestors

In the early years of Christian mission to Africa, it was not uncommon for missionaries to adopt the view that Africans were worshipping their ancestors. Especailly amongst tribes where the Supreme Being occupied a position somewhat distant from the experience of the tribe, the ancestors naturally played a significant and obvious role. Misinterpretation was thus easy enough. Even today, there is still debate concerning the role that the ancestors played at that time, as well as their function at present. Be that as it may, I would like to centre attention on what African theologians have written on this subject in recent years.

In 1972, SE Serote emphatically rejected the notion that the ancestors are regarded by Africans as being on a par with God. He clearly regards ancestor veneration as the correct interpretation of the role of the ancestors:

The Christian ancestors are what the church regards as the triumphant host, the cloud of witnesses. These can never be regarded as alternates to Christ, nor as objects of worship with power attributed to them. With the ancestors put and seen in correct perspective, meaningful Christian worship will take root.[23]

A fuller and more scholarly examination is to be found in an article written by JA Nxumalo, according to whom the Zulu and Basotho people regard the ancestors as creatures, not gods. Africans therefore speak to, rather than pray to, the ancestors. He describes the role of the ancestors:

First, ancestors in traditional religion are believed to have power over the living. They can inflict punishment on those who do not show respect and pay homage to them. They can do good for the family and for the members of their lineage. Second it is clear that they are not like God, supreme, in spite of their power over the family and its affairs.[24]

He also says that while the ancestors are seen, amongst the Basotho, as mediators, they are not regarded as being indispensible. He goes on to discuss in some detail how pastors can best respond to celebration rites for the dead as well as to attitudes amongst believers concerning their ancestors, and concludes by saying:

. . . it is clear that all African theologians and pastors of the soul should make constant attempts to 'purify' elements of African traditional religion and incorporate these into Christian Faith for the benefit of the African Christian and . . . the Universal Church.[25]

The most comprehensive and best-argued discussion by a South African on this subject that I have come across is that of Canon Luke Pato.[26] In essence he seeks to show that, properly understood, the idea of ancestor veneration is similar to the Christian concept of the Communion of Saints.

In this discussion Pato seeks to emphasise the qualitative difference between the African veneration of ancestors and worship of God. He points out that many Xhosa-speaking Christians still participate, often privately, in ancestor veneration. Thus, although in the past Western missionaries tended to reject this emphasis on the ancestors as ancestor worship and, therefore, idolatry, it remains a common practice.

Basic to ancestor veneration is a belief in life after death. The dead are simply the departed who have gone to live elsewhere. In the practice of offering libations (pouring a little beer or milk onto the ground) the relationship between the surviving and deceased members of the family is ceremonially maintained. Ancestors may also be appealed to by family members in times of trouble, and may give advice in dreams and visions.

Accordingly, the so-called 'ancestor-worship' is nothing else but an extension into infinite distance of the family activites on earth and a continuation of the social duties towards the dead.[27]

Pato's concern is to help African believers who are suffering from a conflict between their continuing personal veneration of the ancestors and the Church's general attitude of condemnation. This dilemma, he feels, can be resolved by a 'sound development' of the concept of the communion of saints.

The Church in Africa can take over the consciousness of the African people concerning the departed and transpose it into a Christian and ecclesial solidarity which is rooted in a relationship of mankind with Jesus Christ. In this way, through teaching and proclamation of the Gospel, the Church will undoubtedly be for the African Christians a centre of their existence.[28]

Let us examine what this 'sound development' involves. Pato discusses, in some detail, the various usages of the term *Sanctorum Communio* in the context of various creeds and theological writings. He accepts a synthetic approach to the term in which the *sacramental* (fellowship of 'holy things' such as baptism and communion) and the *personal* (holy persons or saints) meanings are integrated.

He sees two major insights involved in a general definition of the Communion of Saints:

One is that the communion of saints is born and sustained through participation in the sacraments which unite the believer with Christ and with all the saints. The other is that the communion of saints extends the fellowship of the Christian society to the saints of all times. That is, all the redeemed, living or departed, by reason of their union with Christ through the sacraments, are in one spiritual fellowship which physical death does not interrupt.[29]

He then turns to the question of whether the *departed* pray for their brethren on earth. This he regards as probable since, as death does not involve the end of consciousness, the departed can be assumed to continue to remember the living in their prayers.[30] But what is the biblical basis for such a practice?

The New Testament is generally silent on this matter except for one instance, which describes what appears to be a prayer of the dead for the living (Rev 6.9ff). In the Apocalypse the prophet sees the souls of the martyrs interceding with God for the speedy punishment of the persecutors of the Church. In the Early Church, however, there are several clear indications of the belief that the dead in Christ pray for the living.[31]

The next issue is that of the *living* praying for the departed. Again, the NT evidence is scarce and controversial. There are passages in 2 Tim 1:18 and in the apocryphal 2 Maccabees 12:39—49. However, in the Patristic literature, there is a great deal more evidence concerning prayers for the dead. The case rests more on material from the writings of churchmen in various historical periods than on the NT itself. Pato admits the paucity of NT evidence but points out that neither is the practice expressly forbidden. He goes on to say that:

The rationale for the invocation of the saints is derived from the human need for active fellowship with the departed. It is in this way that the invocation of the saints serves to concretise the reality of the communion of saints which includes not only those on earth but also those already departed from us.[32]

This does not mean that Pato is advocating the abuses which were associated with the prayers to the saints (as opposed to God) in the Catholic tradition nor the sale of indulgences which sparked off Luther's 95 theses.[33] Rather, he seeks to show that the history of the Church provides a great deal of evidence for these practices which can be regarded as a practical outworking of the belief in the communion of saints.

My own reaction to these arguments is threefold. Firstly, not coming from an Anglican, Catholic or indeed African background, I find the practice of prayer for the dead quite strange and foreign.[34] Secondly, I wonder whether the truth of a mystical union in Christ of believers can be practically experienced. Even though the departed may be aware of us, can they aid us? Or can we, through our prayers, extend the experience of salvation for the believers or, indeed, open up the way of grace for those who died without appropriating Christ's saving work?[35] Finally, and most important, can the practice of prayer for the dead in certain periods of church history outweigh the relative silence of the NT? Having said this, I am conscious that the final word on this subject has yet to be said. Certainly, the issue of ancestor veneration is one which, because of its importance, will be part of the discussions of African theologians in the future, as well as remaining an issue for all African Christians in terms of both their world-view and religious customs. Therefore, it is more the task of African Christians, than it is mine, to deal with these matters and I trust that they will do so with greater validity and success than has hitherto been the case.

Christianity and African Culture

Culture is an essential, but often unconscious, part of people's lives. It is reflected and expressed in the lives of individuals and of communities. By culture, we mean the patterns of individual and corporate responses to life. Culture thus includes world-views, philosophy, language and commonly held beliefs. It incorporates the society's institutions, associations, laws, customs and rituals. It even encompasses its art, music, poetry, entertainment, industry and architecture. Because culture is so all-encompassing and intimately related to the way in which we see life, its significance with respect to Christianity must not be ignored or minimised.

In recent years, the question of culture — cultural norms, world-views, practices and beliefs — has received much attention. Within churches and mission boards this issue has become a subject of research and discussion. It plays a particularly important role in any adequate mission training programme.[36] The reason for this is clear. Since the early missionary penetration into cultures in Africa, South America and Asia, much thought and controversy have surrounded the culture of both the missionary and those living in the 'mission field'. This has been necessary because so many missionaries tended to confuse 'Western' with 'Christian' and thus either failed to communicate the Gospel effectively or alienated their hearers unduly.

On the whole, missionaries today are more aware of their cultural bondage than were their 19th century counterparts. In the African context, Western missionares are more critical of their own home cultures and more open to the value of African culture which was often regarded, in the past, as barbaric and primitive. Doubtless, this is due to factors such as actual changes in cultural practices, extensive historical, archaeological and anthropological studies and because Africans in the 20th century have done much in the way of explaining and defending their cultures.

Besides culture being an essential part of life, and therefore of religion, it is of particular signifiance for the Christian faith. This is because Christianity is by nature both exclusive and all-encompassing. Exclusive because it claims to be the ultimate revelation of God in Jesus Christ as witnessed to by the scriptures and the church. Christ is thus regarded as the Way, Truth and Life. But it is also all-encompassing, because all nations and people are welcomed if they enter through the gate which is Christ. Christianity thus both judges and embraces cultures, and prizes a unity of faith which allows for diversity of expression and experience. For this reason the world's cultural diversity is a great challenge to the Christian faith as it seeks to save and restore people to God's image and purposes.

Clearly then, it is essential that the ramifications of the interaction between Christianity and culture must be clearly understood in order that the Gospel may be able to redeeem and sanctify all the members of the body of Christ.

At the risk of over-simplification, it may be valuable to divide cultural values and practices into three broad categories:

a) Cultural elements which may be foreign to a Western Christian, but acceptable to the Christian faith (such as dance as a form of worship).

b) Practices which are not fully in accordance with God's will but need to be changed over a period of time (such as some traditional forms of the 'rites of passage').[37]

c) Actions which are completely anathema (such as sexual promiscuity and social injustice) which must be repudiated and subject to Church discipline.

Many African theologians are aware of the issues mentioned above and recognise that culture is not simply a neutral category of thought or practice into which the Christian faith can simply be slotted. LJ Sebidi, for example, has argued that cultural ways of acting and thinking must be purified in accordance with Christ's teaching and that a programme of Africanisation must not become an uncritical acceptance of past practices and beliefs.[38] Similarly, EK Mosothoane has said:

> Rather than throw away her superb religious, cultural, social and conceptual treasures which reveal, among other things, her depth of devotion and existential wisdom, her sheer openness to living, let Africa put all these in the service of the Gospel and therefore subject them to the Gospel they are to serve. In so doing, Africa can only be enriched by the Gospel. But if it is to be enriched, it must also be judged by the Gospel.[39]

This process of cultural renewal is not a simple one, for in the past it often happened that new believers took on the external forms of missionary culture (such as European clothing) without necessarily seeing that their own deeper cultural attitudes and practices remained unchanged.

In his book on the Sotho-Tswana, Gabriel Setiloane points to this disturbing factor:

> The main thesis of this study is that, in spite of the acceptance of Christianity through the teaching of the missionaries, the Sotho-Tswana never totally gave up 'mekgwa ya bo-rra rona', ie their traditional customs, beliefs and ways of life.[40]

A few pages further on he continues:

> Sotho-Tswana concepts and ritual have persisted in spite of many years of Missionary and Church opposition . . . ritual and the things that are vital to the 'soul' of the people in their traditional setting . . . have either been 'baptised' into Christianity, after peripheral adjustment, or have, under cover, been kept alive intact.[41]

For these reasons C Kraft emphasises the need for *minimal critical changes* in the world-view of a particular group in favour of *many peripheral changes*.[42] By this he means that a basic change of allegiance is indeed, not just to another religion or culture, but fundamentally to God himself. Once this allegiance is increasingly understood and applied, it will result in a major change in a person's world-view and assessment of what occurs in his life and society. Whereas, at first, transformation may appear slow, it will be deeper and more lasting than that of a convert who is uprooted and removed from his culture or, alternatively, compelled by outside pressure to conform to the standards of another religio-cultural world-view.[43] Kraft also stresses that this task of critical change cannot be accomplished without the leadership and insight of *African* Christian leaders who are able to mediate between biblical revelation and African cultural beliefs and practices.

As far as the principles of the interaction between Christianity and culture are concerned, it can be seen that African theologians seek to reject what is 'incompatible with the Gospel', while affirming the value of worshipping God and living out their faith as Christian Africans.

A matter that has received special attention is healing, including deliverance from evil spirits. Traditionally, Africans see a close relationship between health and religion, for health is regarded as being symptomatic of a correct relationship between people in a community, and between the community and the spirit world. Illness is not merely regarded as a physical disorder, but is viewed holistically, ie by seeing it in the wider social, psychological and spiritual context. According to African tradition, the cause of illness is not limited to physical disorder, but may be attributed also to human ignorance, folly and sin, the breaking of a taboo, offending ancestral spirits or the malicious action of evil spirits.

African theologians, often influenced by Western thought and medicine, have sought to combine the insights of both worlds, arguing that healing must be understood holistically, ie that illness is caused both by physiological disorder as well as by psychological disturbances. They have not simply repudiated Western medicine but tried to re-emphasise the need for spiritual/supernatural and human community healing.[44] According to M Makhaye:

> To treat the physical without reference to the mental or social aspects of health is doomed to failure by its fragmentary partiality: a cure that neglects mind for body, a spiritualism that neglects body for mind, or an individualism that neglects social relationships cannot hope to complete the wholeness we seek in health.[45]

This holistic emphasis is a significant contribution, especially in terms of the growing number of psychosomatic and mental illnesses experienced in modern industrial society.

Communal life is another important aspect of African culture spoken of by African theologians. Although African life has undergone significant changes as a result of urbanisation and Westernisation, the African sense of community and especially of family responsibility is still very much in evidence. Traditional African culture (as was pre-Industrial European culture) is closer to the OT model of the family and nations, and the NT model of the body of Christ, than is modern Western individualism. As Tutu has put it:

> The African would understand perfectly well what the Old Testament meant when

it said 'man belongs to the bundle of life', that he is not a solitary individual.[46]

The individual is indivisibly related to the community and sees himself or herself as part of the whole. As a result African structures of kinship, social relationships, marriage and custom are controlled by the family and tribal heads, although, with the increasing break-down of tribal unity and rural life, traditional patterns of identity and control are no longer as powerful. Tutu, in fact, resists the temptation to romanticise African communal life by saying:

> Of course this strong group feeling has the weaknesses of all communalism; it encourages conservatism and conformity. It needs to be corrected by the teaching about man's inalienable uniqueness as a person. We need both aspects to balance each other.[47]

Here is an opportunity for whites to learn from the cultural experience of Africans in order to begin to appreciate and experience the strong community base of the NT church. We need, for example, to ask ourselves why we should sit in lines of pews while worshipping as a *community* on a Sunday. Are our 'spectator' worship services a sufficient means of expressing either our faith and praise or Christian love and fellowship?

There is thus a need to distinguish which cultural practices can be appropriated and which must be discarded. LJ Sebidi has quoted, with approval, this statement by Cardinal Zoungrana:

> The content of the message is not to be adapted to a given culture: any culture must be purified from those ways of acting and thinking which are obviously incompatible with Christ's teaching . . . Africanisation is not folklore: It goes much further than that; neither is it a systematic exaltation of everything our ancestors have bequeathed to us. They too, made mistakes.[48]

At this point, it may be noted that 'indigenisation' is not to be confused with 'syncretisation'. The first is the process by which Christian faith is made comprehensible to its hearers and then practised in an appropriate and meaningful way. The second is a false adapting of the message of the Gospel in such a way that it becomes comfortable rather than a challenging or transforming fire within a particular culture. As David Bosch has put it:

> Indigenisation means clothing the God of Scripture in the cultural robes of a specific people. Syncretism means redecorating the traditional God in Christian robes.[49]

Not only Africans, but other peoples also, must become more aware of this tendency to supplement the biblical view of God with their own culturally derived notions.[50] Do white Christians question whether Father Christmas and pine trees or the Easter bunny and his eggs are either valid or necessary expressions of a Christian understanding of the incarnation and resurrection of Christ? Or whether gross materialism, together with vague talk about 'Providence' or 'Mother Nature' are not a Western, secular distortion and denial of the God of the Bible?

This warning, sounded by Bosch in 1972 at the Missiological Conference in Mapumolo, is as telling today as it was them, and must be constantly kept in the forefront of theological thinking and patterns of behaviour in church life:

> In all our theologising and in our daily Christian lives we are constantly in danger of adapting God to our own concepts and pre-suppositions, instead of this happening the other way around.[51]

African Theology and Socio-Political Issues

As discussion of the politicisation of Christianity occurs in several places elsewhere in this book, only a few explanatory comments regarding African Theology and politics are necessary in rounding off this chapter.

While the primary emphasis in African Theology other than in South Africa was previously on the particular issues of African traditional religion and culture, this is no longer the case. Younger African theologians are increasingly turning to a consideration of more overtly political issues.

During the period of resistance to colonial rule in this century, the black churches (both 'mission' and 'independent') were, to varying extents, involved in the struggle for independent black rule. However, once independence was gained, church leaders were to a large extent absorbed into the leadership struggles by virtue of their education or their influence. Consequently, whether for altruistic or selfish reasons, many became part of the new elite and, therefore, supporters of the status quo.[52] But, as the initial euphoria began to dissipate, churchmen were again heard speaking out against the injustices being perpetrated in black-ruled states.

Statements of censure by churchmen against exploitation and discrimination have appeared in documents such as the Kinshasa Declaration (1972) and in the Confession of Alexandria, as well as in the activities and pronouncements of the AACC (All African Conference of Churches).[53]

By the time of the 1977 Pan African Conference of Third World Theologians in Accra, African theologians were drawing extensively on the insights of North and Latin American Liberation Theologies. The following points were made in the *Final Communique* of the Conference:

It is our belief that God's demand of the churches in Africa is that they not only oppose any form of oppression and suffering but also sever any alliances, direct or indirect, with the forces of oppression . . . Because oppression is found not only in culture but also in political and economic structures and the dominant mass media, African Theology must also be *liberation* theology.[54]

Not only political but also sexist oppression was denounced, and delegates were urged to serve others by applying the Gospel to the many needs and conflicts of the African continent.

At this point, the contribution and relevance of South African Black Theology is made evident. As already indicated, black South African Christians have long been interested in the Africanisation of Christianity, and in its application to the realities of their socio-economic and political existence. Concern for Africanisation, Black Consciousness and Liberation thus all occur in South Africa. But before Black Consciousness and Liberation are examined, it is necessary to discuss the African Independent Churches, since they are a good example of the practical workings of Africanisation, and they also reflect a degree of socio-political consciousness.

Notes

1 ZJW Kurewa. 'The Meaning of African Theology' *JTSA* 11 (1975) p36. The issues of African identity and theology rose to prominence at the WCC Conference in Bangkok (1972/3) and the WCC Consultation in Accra (1974) as well as at the All African Conference of Churches (AACC) in Lusaka (1974).

2 It is for this reason that D Bosch questions whether John Mbiti (in his *Concepts of God in Africa*) is correct to assume that there is 'one Supreme God' in Africa. He asks whether the religious beliefs of the some 270 tribes which are discussed can be codified into a simple consistent doctrine of God: cf D Bosch, 'God in Africa: implications for the Kerygma' *Miss* 1:1 (1973) pp3—20.

3 See G Setiloane, *The Image of God among the Sotho-Tswana* (Rotterdam: AA Balkema, 1976) pp89—157; S Gqubule, 'What is Black Theology?' *JTSA* 8 (1974) pp17—19; D Thebahali, 'Has Christianity any relevance for and future among Black people in South Africa?' (unpublished paper) pp1—5. For an excellent discussion by an American (theologian, anthropologist and missionary) on the interaction between biblical revelation and culture both in the way in which the Bible was written and is interpreted, see C Kraft, *Christianity in Culture* (Maryknoll, New York: Orbis Books, 1979) pp169—253.

4 D Tutu, 'Whither African Theology?' in E Fasholé-Luke, *et al* (eds), *Christianity in Independent Africa* (London: Rex Collings, 1978) p366.

5 D Tutu, 'God — Black or White?', *Ministry* 11:4 (1971) p111.

6 M Buthelezi, 'An African Theology or a Black Theology?' in B Moore (ed), *The Challenge of Black Theology in South Africa* pp31ff.

7 J Campbell, *Travels in South Africa* (London: Black, Parry/Routledge and Kegan Paul, 1815) p513. Cf also D Tutu, 'Some African Insights and the Old Testament' *JTSA* 1 (1972) p16ff.

8 D Tutu, 'Whither African Theology?' *op cit,* pp364—366.

9 Quoted in E Fasholé-Luke, 'What is African Christian Theology?' *Com Via* 17 (1974) p101.

10 IK Shuuya, 'An Encounter between the New Testament and African Traditional Concepts' in H-J Becken (ed), *Relevant Theology for Africa* (Durban: Lutheran Publishing House, 1973), p47. Cf also D Tutu, 'Some African Insights and the Old Testament' *JTSA* 1 (1972) p19, which points out the similarities between African and Hebrew understandings of God and society.

11 African Theology in South Africa could benefit from an analysis of the precise nature of God's revelation *outside* the Judaeo-Christian tradition as well as the implications of this revelation for a Christian doctrine of salvation. Whilst these issues have been much discussed, for example in the context of Comparative Religious Studies, they have not received sufficient attention from South African black theologians.

12 SP Legida, 'A Relevant Theology (A Critical Evaluation of Previous Attempts)', in H-J Becken (ed), *A Relevant Theology for Africa* p.31.

13 GM Setiloane, 'Where are we in African Theology?' in K Appiah-Kubi and S Torres (eds), *African Theology En Route*(Maryknoll, New York: Orbis Books, 1979), p60. He is referring here to Christian Gaba (Ghana) and Sam Kibicho (Kenya). See also his 'Modimo: God amongst the Sotho-Tswana' *JTSA* 4 (1973) p17.

14 GM Setiloane, 'Theological Trends in Africa' *Miss* 8:2 (August 1980) p52.

15 For writers outside South Africa who stress a more biblically orientated approach see: E Fasholé-Luke, 'The Quest for African Christian Theologies' in GH Stransky and TF Anderson (eds), *Mission Trends No 3* (Grand Rapids: Eerdmans, 1976) pp136—150; J Mbiti, 'The Biblical Basis for Present Trends in African Theology' in K Appiah-Kubi and S Torres (eds), *African Theology en Route*, pp83—95; K Dickson, 'Towards a *Theologia Africana*' in Mark E Glasswell and EW Fasholé-Luke (eds) *NT Christianity for Africa and the World*, pp198—208; and Byang H Kato, 'Christianity as an African Religion' *Ev RT* 4:1 (1980) pp31—39.

16 S Gqubule, 'What is Black Theology?' *JTSA* 8 (1974) p17

17 S Gqubule, *ibid*, p17. For a further discussion of African and biblical concepts of God by writers outside South Africa, see J Mbiti, *Concepts of God in Africa* (London: SPCK, 1970) and EB Idowu, *Olódùmanè: God in Yoruba Belief* (London: Longmans, 1962).

18 D Bosch, 'God in Africa: Implications for the Kerygma' *Miss* 1:1 (1973) pp3—20.

19 D Bosch, *ibid,* pp12ff. He shows how, in relation to the Canaanite gods such as El and Baal or the Greek Unknown God, the God of the Bible adapts some views, and replaces others, in the process of his self revelation (pp15ff). A Hastings makes a similar point when he speaks of the need for both 'empathy and analysis' in his *African Christianity* (London: Geoffrey Chapman, 1976) p51.

20 M Mabona, 'Black People and White Worship' in B Moore (ed), *The Challenge of Black Theology in South Africa*, p107.

21 A Hastings, *A History of African Christianity 1950—1975,* p235.

22 D Tutu, 'Whither African Theology?' in E Fasholé-Luke, *et al* (eds) *Christianity in Independent Africa,* p369. Concerning dance and song as forms of worship, teaching and evangelism, see G Setiloane, *The Image of God among the Sotho-Tswana* pp156—7.

23 SE Serote, 'Meaningful Christian Worship for Africa' in H-J Becken (ed), *Relevant Theology for Africa,* p150.

24 JA Nxumalo, 'Christ and the Ancestors in the African World: A Pastoral Con-

sideration' *JTSA* 32 (1980) p10. See also E Fasholé-Luke, 'Ancestor Veneration and the Communion of Saints' in Mark E Glasswell and EW Fasholé-Luke (eds) *NT Christianity for Africa and the World*, pp209—221.

25 JA Nxumalo, *ibid*, p21.

26 The work referred to is his MA thesis (submitted in 1980 to the University of Manitoba, Canada) which is entitled: 'The Communion of Saints and Ancestor Veneration: A study of the concept "Communion of Saints" with special reference to the Southern African Religious Experience' by LLL Pato. Another thesis (an MTh submitted by MT Lungu to the University of South Africa, 1982) also deals with this subject under the title 'Xhosa Ancestor Veneration and the Communion of Saints'. He provides a great deal of information regarding Xhosa tradition and biblical texts, but, on the whole, his argument is diffuse and a host of typographical and grammatical errors detract from the impact of his discussion.

27 L Pato, *ibid*, p83.

28 *Ibid*, p98.

29 *Ibid*, pp36—37.

30 This assumption will not of course be acceptable to those who propound the theory of 'soul sleep' (that the person remains unconscious of reality until the point of the final resurrection of the dead). For a discussion of the intermediate state see Stephen H Travis, *Christian Hope and the Future of Man* (Leicester: Inter-Varsity Press, 1980) p111—112.

31 L Pato, *op cit*, p49.

32 *Ibid*, p54.

33 For a discussion of the objections to prayers for the dead see L Pato, *ibid*, pp64—72.

34 In the Anglican Church the practice of invocation continued for a time but in the '10 Articles' of 1536, believers were warned not to confuse honouring the saints in heaven and praying to or worshipping God. Also, discussion of the Doctrine of Purgatory was forbidden. In subsequent revisions of the Book of Common Prayer in 1549, 1562 and 1928, mention of the dead has been in the form of commemoration rather than prayer on their behalf. Nevertheless, Anglican theologians such as Charles Gore and William Temple have spoken in favour of prayers for the dead on the grounds that the dead are mystically united to the living because they are part of the body of Christ. See Pato, *ibid*, pp56—63.

35 Pato refers at this point to the writings of the Catholic theologian Karl Rahner concerning 'the anonymous Christian'. See 'Why and how can we Venerate the Saints?' *Theological Investigations* 8:8 (London: Darton, Longman and Todd, 1971) pp3—23.

36 For an excellent and enlightening discussion of these questions see the work of C Kraft, *Christianity in Culture*, especially pp45—168. The book is particularly helpful in relation to a rural context although its value is not limited to the rural situation.

37 For a discussion of the need to adapt and Christianise African 'rites of passage' see TD Verryn, 'Rites of Passage' in H-J Becken, *Relevant Theology for Africa*, pp139—147.

38 LJ Sebidi, 'Encounter of African Religion with Christianity', *Pro Veritate* (May 1977) p14.

39 EK Mosothoane, 'The Message of the New Testament seen in African Perspective' in H-J Becken, *A Relevant Theology for Africa*, p62.

40 G Setiloane, *The Image of God among the Sotho-Tswana*, p161. For a more re-

cent discussion of the interrelationship between Christianity and African life see J Mosala, 'African Traditional Beliefs and Christianity' *JTSA* 43 (1983) pp15—24.

41 *Ibid*, p185.

42 C Kraft, *op cit*, p362.

43 *Ibid*, pp345—381.

44 The African Independent Churches have been very active in this area of ministry, as will be described in chapter four.

45 MM Makhaye, 'Sickness and Healing in African Perspective' in H-J Becken, *Relevant Theology for Africa* p159.

46 D Tutu, 'Some African Insights and the Old Testament' *JTSA* 1 (1972) p20. Cf also B Goba, 'Corporate-Personality: Ancient Israel and Africa', in B Moore (ed) *The Challenge of Black Theology in South Africa*, pp65—73.

47 *Ibid*, p20.

48 LJ Sebidi, 'Encounter of African Religion with Christianity' *Pro Veritate* (May, 1977) p14.

49 D Bosch, 'God through African Eyes' in H-J Becken (ed) *Relevant Theology for Africa*, p77. Cf also JDY Peel, 'The Christianisation of African Society: some possible models' in E Fasholé-Luke, *et al* (eds), *Christianity in Independent Africa*, pp443—454.

50 See the discussion on hermeneutics (interpretation) in chapter six.

51 D Bosch, 'God through African Eyes' in H-J Becken, *Relevant Theology for Africa,* p72.

52 A Hastings, 'African Christianity (London: Geoffrey Chapman, 1976), Chapter 5 and especially pp90—91. Also see his *A History of African Christianity: 1950—1975*, pp131ff and 184ff.

53 Cf E Fasholé-Luke, 'The Quest for African Christian Theologies', in GH Anderson and TF Stransky (eds), *Mission Trends No 3* pp132—4 and the Kinshasa Declaration *IRM* 61 (1972) pp115—116.

54 Cf K Appiah-Kubi and S Torres (eds), *African Theology en Route* pp191 and 194.

CHAPTER FOUR

African Independent/
Indigenous Churches

As was indicated in chapter one, the African Independent Churches (AICs) have played an important role in the Africanisation of Christianity. Doubtless some of them could be more accurately described an syncretic, but this would certainly be too simplistic as a general interpretation of this often diverse and important movement.[1]

The 19th Century Establishment of the AICs

According to Bengt Sundkler, who was for many years a missionary in Zululand and elsewhere, secessions were not a feature of the period between 1835 and 1885. This, he argues, was a result of the American Mission Board policy of African self-support and self-propagation in the Zulu Church as well as Bishop Colenso's influence amongst the Anglicans,[2] of whom it has been said,

> With regard to his missionary policies, Colenso was convinced that the way forward was not to reject African religions, traditions and customs out of hand, as other missionaries tended to do, but to leaven African culture and its social system with the Gospel . . .[3]

In the latter part of the 19th century, however, this situation began to change. Many Africans had gone to work at the diamond and the gold diggings, and the mission societies could no longer concentrate almost exclusively on the rural population. Many new missionary societies began to operate in the urban areas and large numbers of black Christians were able and willing to assume the mantles of spiritual leadership for the thousands of Africans in 'town'.[4] Meanwhile, as Etherington argues, in the rural areas the decisive factor in religious secession was the increasing restrictions on Africans in terms of land ownership, job opportunities and salaries.[5]

The first secession in South Africa was probably the split within the Paris Evangelical Mission in Basutoland in 1872.[6] Another early secession was led by Nehemiah Tile, who had been ordained in the Wesleyan Methodist Church in 1880, but left and formed his own church in 1884, following a disagreement with his European overseer concerning Tile's involvement in tribal and political affairs. As Sundkler points out:

> The cause of this important secession was not only opposition to European control, but also a positive desire to adapt the message of the Church to the heritage of the Tembu tribe.[7]

The first secession on the Witwatersrand was that of Mangena M Mokone of the Wesleyan Church in Pretoria in 1892. This secession rested, to some extent, on racial grounds. Mokone strongly objected to the church holding two separate Conferences for black and white church leaders. He was also concerned for the evangelisation of the Witwatersrand and the 'self-government of the African Church under African leaders'.[8]

These three examples indicate some of the reasons for secession as well as important concerns which were subsequently to characterise the African Independent Churches. It is possible to see these movements as early forms of what became known as African and Black Theology, because such issues as African culture and beliefs, as well as resistance to white overlordship (religious and political) are clearly evident.

The Phenomenal Growth of the AICs

A major reason why the Independent Churches cannot be excluded from a discussion of the Africanisation of Christianity is their numerical strength. Exact figures are hard to come by, but West has estimated that Independent Churches multiplied as follows:

1913	30
1939	600
1955	1286
1960	2200
1970	3000[9]

Dr HW Turner estimated in 1969 that some 6 million of the 43 million Christians in Africa were members of African Independent Churches.[10] The 1960 census revealed that 21 per cent of black South Africans were members of the

AICs, whereas in 1970 the figure was 18,3 per cent.[11] Although this indicated a percentage drop, the overall number of members has nevertheless grown. By 1970, approximately 3000 AICs were to be found in South Afica, with a membership of some 3,5 to 4 million people. By 1975, in Soweto alone, there were some 900 AICs, varying from fewer than 10 members to more than 200 000. The latter is the Zion Christian Church whose members' badges are often prominently displayed. At the ZCC annual festivals at Zion City Moria, crowds of well over 50 000 people are not exceptional.[12]

Bengt Sundkler's classic study of the AICs, *Bantu Prophets in South Africa*, divides them into two basic groups: Ethiopians and Zionists.[13] The *Ethiopians* take their name from Ps 68.31 ('Ethiopia shall stretch her hands out to God') and Acts 8.27, the account of the conversion of the Ethiopian eunuch. Although they do not all use this name, the Ethiopian churches are typified by the fact that have seceded from white churches for various reasons: racial (they used the slogan of 'Africa for the Africans') and political (in that they were reacting against white power and discrimination in church and society). In most cases, they continued with the patterns of leadership and church policy that they had experienced in the mission churches, except of course, that their leaders were now black. By the start of the 20th century significant numbers of these churches were being founded.

The *Zionist* churches, although they claimed to originate from Mt Zion in Jerusalem, had nothing to do with Jewish Zionism. They were not breakaways from white churches or missionary societies, but tended to be African religious reactions to the disintegration of their traditional societies and power bases. As NA Etherington puts it:

> The destruction of the Zulu power, the British annexation of the Transkei, and the steady erosion of chiefly independence in Natal were body-blows which defenders of the old order tried to parry with new religious weapons . . . Fairly direct connections can be demonstrated between last ditch defences of traditional society and the appearance of tendencies towards Zionism.[14]

According to Sundkler, the Zionist churches were more inclined to a syncretism of Christianity and traditional African religious ideas than were the Ethiopians, as well as being strongly 'nativistic'. Although this was true at the outset of the development of the AICs it is perhaps not so true today. Martin West's study of the AICs in Soweto (published in 1975) suggests that although the original distinction between Ethiopian (as a breakaway from a mission church) and Zionist (as an independetly established church) is still useful, these churches have many similar characteristics. These include, with some variation of incidence, healing, river baptism, dancing, prophets, night communication and drums. He says:

This is broadly the position for all the independent churches in Soweto: a continuum exists, with perhaps most churches falling towards one end or the other — but any simple division would not be entirely accurate, as the variety of churches found within the independent church movement precludes easy classification.[15]

Over the years, many causes have been cited for the founding of the AICs.[16] The reason for their diversity is simply that there are so many of these churches (approximately 6000 in Africa), and because they have been formed over a period of time in many different areas. Although these causes can be categorised into general groups, oversimplification can only be avoided if it is remembered that, with regard to Southern Africa, we are dealing with some 3000 groups.

The establishment and growth of the AICs must be seen in the context of the great impact of Western power and Christianity and the resultant societal dislocation. The unity of African tribal life had been irretrievably shattered, and, with increasing urbanisation, the structures of tribe and family were profoundly affected.

Probably the most important and direct causes of the Independency movement in South Africa were missionary paternalism, racism, inflexibility and misunderstanding on the one hand, and, on the other, the increasingly discriminatory socio-political and economic position in which Africans found themselves.

The vast majority of missionaries did not regard their function as essentially 'self-annihilating', ie a temporary position of ascendency and leadership. Thus, very little was actually done in terms of adequate training and entrusting leadership to African Christians of ability. The secessions of Nehemiah Tile in 1872 and Mokone in 1892 were to a large extent reactions to the missionary attempts to remain rulers instead of becoming guides and partners. Together with their reluctance to relinquish control, whites also failed sufficiently to understand, and respond wisely to, the culture within which they ministered.[17]

The missionary emphasis on 'one soul conversion', which took insufficient account of the community life of the tribe, also caused serious problems. Some Africans refused to be converted because they felt that this amounted to abandoning loyalty to their tribe. Others, having been converted, in fact secretly maintained several tribal beliefs and practices. This resulted in a dual and compartmentalised life. It also meant that within believing communities, Christian transformation and commitment did not necessarily ensue.

Perhaps the most important aspect of the conflict between Africans and missionaries arose over what was to be regarded as 'essentially Christian' and 'merely Western'. For example, there were numerous disputes, in South Africa and elsewhere, regarding polygamy, circumcision, rites of passage (eg birth, puberty, marriage and death), baptism, etc.[18] Interestingly enough, especially with regard to marriage, polygamy is seldom encouraged in the AICs today and many even demand strict monogamy from their followers.[19] Another aspect of the conflict centred around the desire on the part of African Christians to worship in a way that expressed their own culture, needs and Christian experience. This was especially important in a context of social dislocation and political dispossession. Because of their foreignness and association with colonial power, white missionaries could not meet the pastoral needs of their converts in the same way that African leaders could.

Many of the leaders of these early AICs had little, if any, formal theological education, and their congregations were often semi-literate or illiterate. In some of those churches there was (and is) a degree of misunderstanding of the relation between the OT and NT. The NT was often seen as 'the white man's Bible' whereas Africans, who found it easier to relate to the cultural context of the OT, regarded the latter as more important. In many cases, sacrifices, polygamy, refusal to eat pork, etc, were common features of Church life.

Although these religious reasons were significant for the formation of the AICs, other aspects must not be overlooked. There were socio-economic reasons such as the Land Act of 1913 and the Mines and Works Amendment Act (Colour Bar Act) of 1926, which severely restricted Africans with respect to land ownership and farming, as well as upward mobility in the industrial and commercial spheres.[20]

During the late 19th century, a black South African peasantry had slowly begun growing. It grew crops, transported goods and owned property. However, by the 20th century, these opportunities and rights had been eroded by white occupation of land. In addition, legislation restricted blacks to certain reserves, refused them the opportunity to buy land, curtailed their business activities and imposed additional taxation.[21]

Politically also, Africans were restricted in that they were allowed no effective representation in the central government, and the limited tribal authority of the few remaining chiefs was further subject to the Native Administration authoritites.

Moreover, 'native' pastors were paid far less than their white counterparts and, indeed, far less than blacks in farming, business and skilled trades. Thus, not only were these pastors continually restricted in terms of church leadership or in expressing initiative in evangelism, but their families also suffered because of the poor salaries they earned.[22] Etherington has said this regarding the Nguni people (mainly Zulus):

> It was no coincidence that African interest in Church leadership rose in inverse proportion to the decline in opportunities for other sorts of leadership. By the bitterest of ironies each generation of Black Christians was better equipped than the last to compete with white settlers but was prevented from doing so by laws which

grew progressively severe. Since there was a limited number of attractive ec-
clesiatical positions available, Africans were inspired to create new positions by
forming new Churches.[23]

The AICs thus provided compensation for the loss of self-determination and
acted as an outlet for dissatisfaction and frustration. Many of these groups
also embodied hopes for an apocalyptic restructuring of society and expecta-
tions of a black Messiah.[24]

It can be seen that it is difficult to separate the religious and political
elements in the establishment and growth of the AICs. Clearly, there were
religious reasons such as the interpretation of the Bible, forms of worship,
evangelism, leadership opportunities, etc. There were, however, also political
reasons such as African reactions to the loss of land, restrictions on labour,
salaries and social mobility.

There were also other, less important, causes. The prevalence of denominationalism was a signficiant, though perhaps indirect, reason for secession. In
areas where there were a large number of missionary groups at work, the unity
of Christianity was already compromised in African eyes. This was intensified
in those places where strife and 'sheep-stealing' were a feature of missionary
activity. Together with the divisive influence of denominationalism, went the
indigenous divisions of tribalism. When PJ Mzimba left the Lovedale
Presbyterian Church early in this century, for example, only the Fingo
members accompanied him, while the Xhosa remained behind.[25]

Having dicussed the reasons for the establishment of the AICs and indicated
their phenomenal growth, we now proceed to an an examination of the value
and importance of the Independent Churches.

Contribution of the AICs

During the last 15 years, there has been a change in the way in which the AICs
are evaluated. This trend stands in sharp contrast to some of the earlier
criticisms, even rejections, of the African separatist movement. This criticism
was voiced in the *Christian Express* (April, 1897):

> Now we come to the serious portion of the history of this new Native Church, and
> the new danger it is creating. Had it been true to its name and original profession
> as a genuine product of South African native growth, and had it shown itself to be
> a missionary church ready to work in districts yet unevangelised it might have call-
> ed for some sympathy . . . Instead of helping to solve this important question, this
> Ethiopian church seems to have resolved iself into an agency for importing another
> denomination into the South African mission field.[26]

Some even went so far as to condemn the movement out of hand, accusing it of syncretism, schism and fanaticism. They were alarmed at practices such as dancing and prophecy and felt that these churches boded only ill for the future of Christianity. Not everyone, however, shared these negative views. Another editorial in the *Christian Express* (June, 1906) recognised that:

> It may be that the Missionary Churches have been slow to recognise that the Native Church is quickly leaving its childhood behind, and is able to take upon itself an increased measure of self control. It is conscious of new powers and is impatient of dictation.[27]

Many years later, Bengt Sundkler published his pioneering book, *Bantu Prophets in South Africa* (1948, 1961), which contained a wealth of information and discussion. In 1964 there followed Marie-Louise Martin's *Biblical Concept of Messianism and Messianism in South Africa*, and in 1968 *Post-Christianity in Africa* by GC Oosthuisen.[28] Both books tended to be critical of the AICs and Oosthuisen interpreted them to be 'post-Christian' rather than valid African expression of Christianity. He proposed a threefold classification of Churches, Christian Sects and Nativism, with the vast majority of the AICs in the latter two groups. These books were followed by many more dealing with other parts of Africa as well as a great number of articles. In these more recent studies the tide of opinion has swung in favour of the AICs.

Thus, James Kieran has criticised both Sundkler and Oosthuisen for characterising the AICs as essentially 'nativistic' movements.[29] Indeed Sundkler himself later began to see the AICs in a more positive light. More and more it was admitted that it was hardly honest to criticise the AICs for being too closely tied to their indigenous culture if the European churches were being rejected by the AICs for this very fault of 'cultural captivity'. De Gruchy sums up:

> All that is required here is to note that the African Independent churches were increasingly recognised as legitimate expressions, by and large, of Christian faith in Africa, and as legitimate protests against many of the spiritually deadening influences in the more traditional [mission] churches.[30].

One of the scholars in the forefront of this new evaluation is Dr HW Turner of Aberdeen University, Scotland. According to him, the ability of the AICs:

> to synthesise traditional forms and values with new modes of life and organisation, and to do so within the new historical mode of thought, makes the independent churches important agents of modernisation, yet accommodated to their members' readiness for change, and cushioning the impact upon them of the disturbing forces from the outside world.[31]

Turner sees the AICs elsewhere in Africa as mediating between the forces of tradition and the forces of change, rather than merely negating them as examples of syncretism or fanaticism.

As has been pointed out, the AICs were formed in a context of dispossession and change. In the urban areas this was compounded by the alien environment of the city with its accompanying turmoil and rootlessness. The search for identity, security and friendship was an immensely powerful psychological (and spiritual) driving force. People found, much to their disappointment, that many of their needs could not be, and were not, met by the mission churches. Thereafter, they found their spiritual homes in the various Independent Churches which provided teaching, healing, fellowship, active worship, comfort and encouragement. The smaller congregations provided both more personal communication and opportunities for leadership. All of this adds up to the fact that these Independent Churches *ministered* to each other and to the newcomers who sought them out. As Sundkler puts it:

> In a world of disintegration, danger and disease, they all claim to function as a refuge of health and wholeness. Healing is the need of their fellowmen, and this they all attempt to provide. With this, they give to uprooted and lonely men and women the warm fellowship and loving concern — not seldom by way of tactile expression — which they are seeking.[32]

The AICs have also successfully bridged tribal affiliations. West's study of Sowetan Independent Churches has produced ample evidence of people from Zulu, Sotho, Xhosa, Swazi, Pedi, Ndebele and other backgrounds who are members of multi-tribal churches. Services are often conducted in two or three languages, as well as including additional interpretations at salient points.[33]

The AICs have provided comfort and counsel to Africans in areas where other churches have been unable to help. This is evidenced especially clearly in the issues of witchcraft and evil-spirit possession. Amongst urban Africans the fear of being bewitched is in fact increasing. This is because different tribes and families are being forced to live in close association, and when tragedy strikes the tension between individuals and groups rises significantly. The traditional mission churches have little ability to cope with this need. Either they reject the idea of witches and bewitching altogether, or they do not regard it as a necessary part of the church's task to deal with it.[34] In contrast, the AICs provide mechanisms for 'witchsmelling' and the inducement of confession of sins previously unconfessed. In the service, the leaders, often under inspiration, accuse various individuals, or the group as a whole, of misbehaviour. At this point confessions of sorcery and sin pour out, and the guilty individuals are exposed to repentance, forgiveness and healing.[35]

The AICs place a great emphasis on disease and healing. Because they do not have a Western physiological, cause/effect approach to health, illness may be blamed on other people or the ancestors, any of which may be making use of agencies such as the weather, germs, events, etc. The primary question regarding illness is not 'what is it?' but 'who sent it, and why?'

> The African will not deny the efficacy of Western medicine, but usually will insist that it deals only with the physical and symptomatic aspects of the illness. It never deals with the cause. It is unconcerned with the who and the why. For this reason Africans frequently say that Western medicine leaves the spiritual dimension of illness completely untouched.[36]

Lowen also discusses the way in which the AICs provide 'cities' of refuge and healing, supply the various community and fellowship needs of believers, and encourage a holistic view of salvation by assisting members to relate their faith to the world. In particular, the AICs seem to draw members rather than, as he puts it, 'beating the bush' for converts.[37]

Besides the extremely important areas of fellowship and healing, their vitality of worship and prayer provides the AICs with much of their character and attraction. Prophets, healers, evangelists, preachers and large choirs all play an important part in the atmosphere of praise and adoration that is the essence of their services. Emotion, dancing, loud singing and possession of the Spirit may contrast with the generally staid Anglo-Saxon approach (especially in 'non-Charismatic' churches). But the genuineness of the worship and prayer, rather than their particular cultural expression, should surely be the test. In this the various commentators are agreed. Both West and Sundkler, for example, refer to the vigils kept by the vast majority of AICs at Easter time. In a service that lasts 18 hours, the Apostolic Full Gospel Mission of South Africa (in Soweto), sings, prays, accepts new members, ordains officers, enjoys a communal meal, and worships by holding a long vigil on Good Friday. Sundkler, writing of the Christian commitment of the Zionist churches during the Holy Week from Good Friday to Easter Morning says that:

> These services show an intense identification in witness and song on the part of almost every man and woman present, with the drama on Calvary and with the Man of Sorrows. Nobody has the right to cry 'Syncretism' here, whatever the peculiar denominational paraphernalia may have been.[38]

Another important issue concerning the AICs is that of education and theological training. West notes that the majority of bishops, presidents and preachers (ie the top leaders) of the Soweto AICs do not have much in the way of formal education. However, they have usually completed some basic bible correspondence courses. There is a strong emphasis on the Bible as the Word of God, usually accompanied by a fundamentalist interpretation. For this reason, they have responded positively to further bible teaching and training, such as offered at one stage by AICA (African Independent Churches Association) and at present by groups such as TEE (Theological Education by Extension). This would seem an important area of future growth and one to which others can contribute, as is being done at present by Mennonite missionaries in the Transkei. Instead of condemning the AICs for emotionalism, syncretism or ignorance, sound biblical teaching, sensitive to the strengths and needs of the AICs, and an emphasis on the Triune God of Christian faith would go a long way towards solving any problems whilst building on existing foundations. Therefore, in replying to the question, 'Is it possible to help the AICs become more biblical while continuing to meet the needs of African Christians?', Lowen provides an emphatic *yes*[39]

The AICs and Social Transformation

At present, the AICs in South Africa generally do not take any specific or aggressive political line. According to Turner, because blacks are denied a significant share in the central government structure and are unable to express political criticism freely, they tend to shy away from political expression, refusing to 'rock the boat' and bring down the ire of the authorities upon their heads.

> In consequence some of the churches show an uncritical acceptance of the political powers, and are prepared to co-operate with the government and its apartheid policy while continuing much as a traditional ontocratic society amongst themselves.[40]

This quiescence has, however, not always been the norm, for there were distinctly political, even seditious elements in the preaching of the earlier AICs. Although this was perhaps not as widespread as some Europeans imagined or feared, it did exist.

For example, the Bambata Rebellion of 1906 was marked by seditious preaching among the Ethiopian groups who proclaimed that there should be an African ascendancy over whites. Also, in the tragic incident at Bulhoek (near Queenstown) in 1921, the potential for religiously inspired resistance to the government was evidenced. The leader of the movement, Enoch Mgijima, had established a religious community of a few hundred members. They were ordered by the authorities to move since they were squatting on Crown Land. Despite several warnings, Mgijima refused to budge and told his people that the army's bullets would be turned to water. On his order, about 500 of his followers charged the machine guns of the troops and over 150 were needlessly and callously killed.[41]

Elsewhere in Africa, for example in Kenya and Tanganyika (now Tanzania), the association of indigenous church movements and nationalism was even more prevalent and also more successful in resisting white overlordship. A comparison has been drawn by Robert J Janosik between the Kenyan and South Africa contexts, with respect to the religio-political dynamic of the AICs. He compares the various Kikuyu associations in Kenya (from the 1920s to the Mau-Mau of the 1950s) with movements amongst the Zulus of South Africa.[42] Whereas in Kenya these associations, including churches, were able to destabilise colonial authority, in South Africa they were not so successful. He does not attribute this, as others have done, only to the strength of white power, but to different leadership structures in the Kikuyu and Zulu Independent Church structures. Amongst the Kikuyu, leaders were willing to delegate power and use other leaders and, as a result, the group was more inclined to have an ongoing influence on societal affairs. In contrast,

> among the Zulu, the picture is one of intrasect squabbling, secessionist struggles, adjustment to the rigidities of the white regime, and a distinct effort to avoid head-on clashes with white political powers. A few anomic exceptions notwithstanding, the message of the Zulu sects and churchmen has been one of political deference and quiescence.[43]

The political reticence of the AICs may also be explained by the fact of overwhelming white power in the socio-political sphere. Military resistance was foolhardy and sabotage dangerous; by the late 1920s, by and large, resistance had died out, and the AICs concentrated on building up their churches and extending their influence amongst their fellow Africans.

As late as the 1950s this political reticence remained a feature of the AICs, as a result of their intense desire to obtain registration papers and official recognition. These requirements were part of the government's attempts to establish greater control, in all spheres, in the fast growing urban areas. Registration was relatively easy to come by, but official recognition was certainly not. By this time only 81 churches had received offical sanction and the others were threatened with the possibility of removals or dissolution, since without recognition no township sites could be granted to churches.[44] The result was a frantic attempt to secure association with recognised Independent (or even mission) churches and to reapply for recognition. Most did not receive it and thus resorted to meeting in houses, garages, open spaces near rivers, and even hiring school classrooms.

More recently, there have been indications that this political quiescence may be changing. Victor Mayatula, of the Bantu Bethlehem Christian Apostolic Church of Africa,

. . . is one of those who are convinced that an authentic expression of what Black Theology is really about is to be found precisely in these churches. Black Theology is concerned with Liberation; this is also the concern of the Independent Churches. In the Ethiopian and Messianic churches, he says, the emphasis is on physical liberation, in the Zionist churches it is on psychological liberation. He therefore sees a miracle taking place today: a large group of young black intellectuals are placing their hope in the Independent Churches.[45]

There is no doubt that as a result of the importance of the AICs and the recent more positive evaluations of them, they will become more attractive to young blacks. They could also become vehicles of cultural needs and political inspirations. If this is so, the present character of the AICs may well change. This would, however, require several changes of thought and direction, since the vast majority of AIC leaders are not inclined to confront the South African situation.

The AICs have previously been active, and are likely to continue to be so, in the socio-economic area. As has already been pointed out, they have often taken pains to provide for the needs of their members. In the urban areas this has meant giving money, helping with funerals, assisting each other to find employment and coping with family crises.[46] They seek to provide their members with encouragement, help and guidance. The AICs have also initiated various social and economic enterprises such as agricultural development, housing and home industries.[47] In the Transkei a start has been made by damming water, improving agricultural methods and generally seeking to provide for some of the needs of the village community.[48]

What role do African women play in all this? Many women hold church office as a consequence of their husbands being office bearers. For example, there are Lady Bishops. There are also such elected officers as Chairlady, Organiser, Secretary and Treasurer. In the *manyano* (women's services), these women meet regularly and are often the 'backbone' of the Church.[49] The influence of these women is not, however, restricted to the *manyano* groups. Through the exercise of prophetic gifts, women may directly influence the church. In the Apostolic Full Gospel Mission of South Africa (in Soweto) it is the Senior Prophetess rather than the Lady Bishop who is most influential.[50] It has been pointed out that in East Africa:

> Revival has lifted hundreds of thousands of African women and given them a new role, a new sense of personal worth. I do not know of any other factor in East Africa which to that extent has served to emphasise equality betwen the sexes as Revival.[51]

Christianity, in terms of both the mission and independent churches, has certainly afforded women both new status and responsibility. This is not to say that all women were previously treated as children or chattels, but rather to point out that their worth and contribution to society and the Church has been heightened and appreciated to a greater extent.

All in all, therefore, the AICs represent a vital aspect of the African Christian community, which has already evidenced its desire to formulate and experience an authentic African Christianity and one which, it is hoped, will increasingly succeed in fulfilling this desire.

This brings us to the end of this discussion on the theme of Africanisation in terms of both African Theology and the African Independent Churches. The next step is to concentrate our attention on Black Theology in relation to Black Identity (chapter five) and Black Liberation (chapter six).

Notes

1 This chapter will not attempt to cover all the possible topics or areas of the African Independent Church Movement, but to select certain issues which illustrate and explain the Africanisation of Christianity or relate to its politicisation.

2 B Sundkler, *Bantu Prophets in South Africa* (Oxford: Oxford University Press, 1961) pp25—27.

3 JW de Gruchy, *The Church Struggle in South Africa,* p17.

4 Sundkler, *op cit,* p27ff.

5 NA Etherington, 'The Historical Sociology of Independent Churches in South-East Africa' *JRA* 10:2 (1979) p120ff.

6 GC Oosthuisen, 'Causes of Religious Independentism in Africa' *Ministry* 11:4 (1971) p121.

7 Sundkler, *op cit,* p38. I have heard it said that Nehemiah Tile could be regarded as the first black theologian in South Africa. Unfortunately, not much research has been done on his life.

8 *Ibid,* p38ff.

9 M West, *Bishops and Prophets in a Black City* (Cape Town: David Philip, 1975) p2. The fissiparous tendency (schism and secession) of the Church is not just a recent phenomenon, but has been present for the past 20 centuries. This is mentioned by JB Welbourne, *East African Rebels* (London: SCM, 1961) p165. For a discussion of more recent trends see Andrew F Walls, 'The Challenge of African Independent Churches' *Ev RT* 4:2 (1980) p226ff, and Harold W Turner, 'Survey Article: The Study of New Religious Movements in Africa, 1968—1975', *Religion* (August, 1975) pp88—98.

10 HW Turner, 'The Place of Independent Religious Movements in the Modernisation of Africa,' *JRA* 2:1 (1969) pp43—44.

11 D Bosch, 'Racism and Revolution: The Response of the Churches in South Africa' *Occasional Bulletin of Missionary Research* 3:1 (July 1979), p14.

12 JW de Gruchy, *The Church Struggle in South Africa,* p46; B Sundkler, *Zulu Zion and some Swazi Zionists,* (Uppsala: Gleerups, 1976) p287; and M West, *Bishops and Prophets in a Black City,* pp10, 43—44.

13 B Sundkler, *Bantu Prophets in South Africa*, p38ff. Although some have criticised this distinction, it remains, by and large, an accurate and useful one for the South African situation. Sundkler also had a third category of 'Messianic', which referred to churches that followed a 'Native Messiah'. But, as de Gruchy points out in his *Church Struggle in South Africa*, p45, he later rejected this category as unnecessary and misleading. See also Sundkler's more recent *Zulu Zion and some Swazi Zionists* p308ff. For a recent description of publications regarding the AICs see HW Turner, 'New Studies of New Movements: Some Publications on African Independent Churches since 1973' *JRA* 11:2 (1980) pp137—153.

14 NA Etherington, 'The Historical Sociology of Independent Churches in South-East Africa' *JRA* 10:2 (1979) pp124—5. He supports Sundkler's distinction between Ethiopian and Zionist, but questions the view that Ethiopianism led to Zionism and, thus, to heathenism. Rather, the causes for Ethiopianism must be distinguished from those of Zionism.

15 West, *op cit*, pp19—20.

16 GC Oosthuisen, 'Causes of Religious Independentism', *op cit* pp121—133, lists more than 80.

17 GC Oosthuisen, *Post Christianity in Africa* (London: C Hurst and Co, 1968) p61.

18 On Nigeria see JB Webster, *The African Churches amongst the Yoruba 1888—1922* (Oxford: Clarendon Press, 1964), and on Kenya, FB Welbourne, *East African Rebels* (London: SCM, 1961).

19 M West, *op cit*, p40, and Andrew Walls, 'The Challenge of African Independent Churches', *Ev RT* 4:2 (1980) p232.

20 NA Etherington, *op cit*, p120ff, has provided a significant amount of documentation to indicate that it was primarily the decline of opportunities in the secular sphere and the possibility of leadership in the new churches that opened the way for the proliferation of AICs. He regards this reason as more important than, for example, denominationalism, interpretation of the Scriptures, racial segregation, reluctance to ordain ministers, etc.

21 *Ibid*, pp120—124.

22 *Ibid*, p121ff.

23 *Ibid*, p123.

24 See GC Oosthuisen, *Post Christianity in Africa*, pp76—79.

25 Sundkler, *Bantu Prophets in South Africa* p43.

26 In Francis Wilson and Dominique Perrot (eds), *Outlook on a Century: South Africa 1870—1970* (Johannesburg: Lovedale and Spro-cas, 1972) p154.

27 *Ibid*, p377.

28 M-L Martin, *The Biblical Concept of Messianism and Messianism in Southern Africa* (Morija, 1964), and GC Oosthuisen, *Post Christianity in Africa* (London: C Hurst, 1968).

29 J Keiran, 'Zionist Communion', *JRA* 11:2 (1980) p125, discusses the nature and role of communion services in the AICs.

30 JW de Gruchy, *The Church Struggle in South Africa*, p46.

31 HW Turner, 'The Place of Independent Religious Movements in the Modernisation of Africa' *JRA* 2:1 (1969) p57. See also Andrew F Walls, 'The Challenge of African Independent Churches' *Ev RT* 4:2 (1980) pp225—234.

32 B Sundkler, *Zulu Zion and some Swazi Zionists*, p307.

33 M West, *op cit*, p43.

34 Jacob A Loewan, 'Mission Churches, Independent Churches, and Felt Needs in

Africa', *Missiology: An International Review* 4:4 (October 1976) p410, and G Setiloane, 'How the traditional world-view persists in the Christianity of the Sotho-Tswana' in E Fasholé-Luke *et al* (eds), *Christianity in Independent Africa* p407—8.

35 Loewen, *ibid*, p411ff.

36 *Ibid*, p411.

37 *Ibid*, pp412—424. Loewan provides detailed examples of aspects of the work of the AICs and goes a long way to explain to Westerners practices and beliefs which seem to them at first decidedly odd.

38 B Sundkler, *Zulu Zion and some Swazi Zionists*, p316. Regarding the charge of syncretism, West indicates that some of the AICs vehemently deny that they have contact with the *ancestors* (those who have died) or the *shades* (also those who have died but are able to influence the lives of the living): cf M West, *Bishops and Prophets in a Black City*, pp33, 40 and 45.

39 Loewen, *op cit*, p423.

40 H W Turner, 'The Place of Independent Religious Movements in the Modernisation of Africa', *JRA* 2:1 (1969) p50.

41 West, *op cit*, p4; Sundkler, in *Zulu Zion and some Swazi Zionists* p285 cites the number of people killed as 117.

42 Robert J Janosik, 'Religious and Political Involvement: A Study of Black African Sects', *JSSR* 13 (1974) pp161—175.

43 *Ibid*, p169. He also speaks of the ideological differences; the Zulus tended to have a fixed and static set of beliefs and practices which either stultified the group or resulted in secession. In contrast, the Kikuyu were more tolerant and therefore more flexible. The Kikuyu were also able to recruit more widely and their numbers gave their efforts more weight and influence.

44 Sundkler, *Zulu Zion and some Swazi Zionists* p284.

45 D Bosch, 'Currents and Cross currents in South African Black Theology ' in GS Wilmore and JH Cone (eds), *Black Theology: A Documentary History, 1966—1979*, p228. See also H-J Becken (ed), *Relevant Theology for Africa* pp174—177 for V Mayatula's article. For a recent discussion of the socio-political contribution of the AICs in Zimbabwe see ML Daneel, 'Communication and Liberation in African Independent Churches', *Miss* 11:2 (1983) pp57—93.

46 Cf West, *op cit*, pp22—47 and 194—203. For a recent discussion of the task of the African Church (Both mission and independent) in the cities see B Goba, 'The Role of the Urban Church: A Black South African Perspective', *JTSA* 38 (1982) pp26—33.

47 HW Turner, *op cit*, p59.

48 For example in the work of Mennonites such as the Rev Laurence Hills and some of the staff of the TCC (Transkei Council of Churches).

49 West, *op cit*, p24.

50 *Ibid*, p31.

51 B Sundkler, 'Worship and Spirituality' in E Fasholé-Luke, *et al*, (eds), *Christianity in Independent Africa*, p551. Cf also his *Bantu Prophets in Africa* p139ff and 202ff. The role of women in the AICs was also one of the topics dealt with at the January 1984 Annual Conference of the *SA Missiological Society*.

CHAPTER FIVE

Black Theology and Black Identity

In the USA and in South Africa Black Theology incorporates the themes of Black Consciousness and Black Liberation. Although these two are closely inter-related, they will be discussed in separate chapters, with Black Consciousness forming the subject of this chapter.

The importance of Black Consciousness in the writings of South African black theologians can hardly be overemphasised. Therefore, the relationship between the ideology of Black Consciousness and the content of Black Theology needs to be examined, not only in the light of questions regarding the nature of black solidarity (ie whether it is racist and nationalistic), but also because of the impact of Black Consciousness on the thinking of black theologians.

The Rise of Black Consciousness

According to Steve Biko:

> . . . Black Consciousness is in essence the realisation by the black man of the need to rally together with his brothers around the cause of their oppression — the blackness of their skin — and to operate as a group in order to rid themselves of the shackles that bind them to perpetual servitude.[1]

This thinking, which sought to bind together all the black groups within South Africa in a common pursuit, was a development of the late 1960s. This was not the first time that blacks had sought to challenge white 'superiority' and power. As was indicated in chapter one, black Christians were not silent in the earlier parts of the century.[2] The Black Consciousness Movement of the 60s and 70s must, therefore, be viewed against the background of earlier African nationalism, as well as of protest from within the Coloured and Indian communities.[3] Nevertheless, Black Consciousness was a new departure in that it was a united black rejection of white dominance.

This can be seen in the fact that Black Consciousness was a more inclusive concept than was African nationalism and thus it could draw upon a broader group for both its leaders and members. Moreover, Black Consciousness did not remain limited to a small number of politicised leaders, but was more successful in its attempt to influence the larger mass of people than any other previous black movement in South African history. This is because the Black Consciousness movement

> Provided a bridge across ethnic divisions within the black community, binding in one all African, Coloured and Indian students who rejected separate development and who were striving for alternative ways of combating apartheid.[4]

There were developments elsewhere which also influenced the South African Black Consciousness movement. South African blacks were greatly encouraged by the establishment of independent black rule in other parts of Africa, as well as being influenced by the nationalist ideologies that were at the base of these changes. Ideas such as Negritude (Leopold Senghor), African humanism (Kenneth Kaunda) and self-reliant African socialism (Julius Nyerere) were studied and adapted. Black leaders in South Africa increasingly asserted the value of their identity and culture in the face of the discrimination practised against them.

It was not only from post-colonial Africa that South Africans drew inspiration. The civil rights movement in the USA and the leadership of people such as Martin Luther King also served as models for study and adaptation. There was also the development of Black Theology by Americans such as Cone, Wilmore, and Roberts. James Cone, more than anyone else, has had a major impact on South African Black Theology, through his books and articles, and also as a result of a taped address by Cone played at a 1971 Seminar on Black Theology in Roodepoort. (Prof Cone had been invited to attend but was refused an entry visa by the South African authorities.)

While the importance of Cone's role cannot be ignored and should not be minimised, it does appear to be misleading, if not false, to regard South African Black Theology as an import from the USA.[5] Such an approach takes insufficient account of earlier developments within South Africa and of the thinking of its black leaders. Thus, with respect to SASO (South African Students' Organisation), Gail Gerhart has rightly pointed out:

> To say that SASO's ideology was 'imported' would be to assign much too little significance to the life experiences and political intuition of the movement's

founders: yet . . . never had such a deliberate and thorough-going effort been made to borrow and selectively adapt foreign ideas in order to influence mass thinking.[6]

The immediate historical context of the development of Black Consciousness was the period following the tragedy of Sharpeville in March 1960. These years were marked by a shocked and frustrated silence as organisations such as the African National Congress (ANC) and the Pan Africanist Congress (PAC) were banned, while their members were jailed or harassed. With these avenues of protest and resistance blocked, some blacks became involved in government-created institutions such as the Urban Bantu Councils or rural 'Homelands'. Others went into exile, and several black university students joined the multi-racial NUSAS (National Union of South African Students). Later, however, they became increasingly dissatisfied with its white liberalism and its non-racial antidote to apartheid. As a result, some black students became convinced that it was necessary for them to break away, and to go ahead on their own.

In December 1968, about thirty black NUSAS representatives came together at Mariannhill to analyse their situation. After much discussion, it was decided to form an all-black society to represent black interests, and in July 1969 the first SASO conference was held.

SASO's importance lay in the fact that it was regarded by many as a movement which articulated their hopes and frustrations. It expressed a new mood of unity and self-affirmation amongst black people. Moreover, its impact did not remain restricted to university students, but was extended to both high school students and, through the Black People's Convention (BPC) and the Association for the Educational, Social and Cultural Advancement of African Peoples (ASSECA), to the adult generation.

The Relationship between Black Consciousness and Black Theology

It would be a mistake to regard Black Consciousness as a purely secular movement because, from the outset, it encompassed very definite religious elements and implications.

A year before the formation of SASO, the University Christian Movement (UCM) was founded, in an attempt to establish a Christian student organisation that was not bound by race or denomination.[7] Christian student organisations at that time, especially after the fragmentation of the Students' Christian Association (SCA) into four groups, were divided by race, language, denomination and culture. They lacked a unity of purpose and organisation that could operate across racial and denominational barriers. It was this type of ecumenism that UCM sought to build. UCM also stood against apartheid and some of its leaders were involved in the writing of *The Message to the People of South Africa* (September, 1968).[8]

The UCM was especially active on the campuses of Fort Hare and the Federal Theological Seminary (Fedsem) in the Eastern Cape. Much of the promotion of UCM in that area was the work of Basil Moore, a white Methodist minister. In Johannesburg, the Anglican Chaplain at the University of the Witwatersand, John Davies, sought to co-ordinate UCM's activities and extend its influence. Although the UCM did not achieve all its aims (it had dissolved by 1972), it made a significant contribution, encouraging black Christians to express their thoughts and feelings, and being responsible for setting up a number of seminars on Black Theology. The most important of these seminars was held in Roodepoort in 1971.[9]

While a particularly *theological* emphasis was most evident in the UCM, SASO was not simply a political pressure group. Biko himself had been involved with UCM and many of the members of SASO had been educated in mission schools or were theology students at Fedsem and the Lutheran and Catholic seminaries. The seminarians and university students were, however, not the only ones who were influenced by Black Consciousness; many black churchmen also became increasingly interested in it. Although many black ministers regarded political involvement as something best avoided, they were vulnerable to politicisation because of the political conservatism of the white churches, the differentiation between salaries for black and white churchmen and the lack of leadership opportunities for blacks in the multi-racial churches.

The theological dimension of Black Consciousness thus came to be represented in the form of Black Theology. This was evident in the interrelation between the political *and* theological concerns of many black leaders. These were broadened at conferences and seminars on Black Theology such as those held in Roodepoort and Pietermaritzburg in 1971 and at Hammanskraal in 1972. In addition, at the Black Renaissance Convention held in 1974 two of the eight papers were related to Black Theology.[10]

Any assessment of the relationship between Black Consciousness and Black Theology must, therefore, take cognisance of their interdependency and mutual influence. The Black Consciousness movement certainly roused black theologians to question their theological insights, and impressed upon them the necessity of relating their faith to black self-awareness. Manas Buthelezi wrote in 1973:

> The last three years have been characterised by the evolution of Black Consciousness in South Africa. This in turn called for the need to relate the Christian

faith to the experience of the black man.[11]

Conversely, it is also true that Black Theology provided the Black Consciousness movement with an immensely powerful spiritual foundation and motivation. Blacks were able, on theological grounds, to reject a negation of their humanity as 'inferior' and to affirm the value of their blackness. As Ernest Baartman has expressed it:

> No more is he [the black man] going to try and fit into a non-white portrait drawn by the white man. No more is he going to say what the white man wants to hear and thus continue his own indignity. No more does the white man epitomise all that is good, just and of value . . . Black Consciousness is the black man saying 'yes', he says yes to who he is in Jesus Christ.[12]

Blackness, Racism and Integration

Having dealt with the rise of Black Consciousness and the inter-relationship between it and Black Theology, we need to take a closer look at the actual context and implications of Black Theology.

In Black Theology, the term 'black' can be understood in two ways. Firstly, it refers to all those previously called 'non-whites' or 'non-Europeans', ie Africans, Coloureds and Indians. The emphasis here is on skin-colour. The significance of the use of 'black' lies in the fact that whereas previously blackness was something from which some blacks sought to escape, it has increasingly become a point of self-affirmation. Blackness cannot be viewed as a curse if blacks realise the full implications of being created in the image of God. As Manas Buthelezi has written:

> As long as somebody else says to you, 'You are black, you are black', blackness as a concept remains a symbol of oppression and of something that conjures up feelings of inferiority. But when the black man himself says, 'I am black, I am black', blackness assumes a different meaning altogether. It then becomes a symbol of liberation and self-articulation.[13]

Secondly, 'blackness' is taken to be synonymous with 'the oppressed people in South Africa'. Allan Boesak speaks of blackness as being more than skin-colour, of being both a state of mind or attitude, and a condition of oppression. While it is important to bear in mind the distinction between blackness as skin-colour and as a condition of oppression, in practice the word is used in both senses, often interchangeably, or to mean both at once.

This emphasis on 'blackness' must not be confused with black racism, nor is it a simple case of blackness versus whiteness. It is rather a choice between blackness and nihilism. For, as the poet Adam Small has shown, acquiesence to white donomination has sapped the will of blacks and the equation of whiteness with value is not only false but inherently destructive.[14] Therefore

> Black Theology is an appeal to the black man to overcome his slave mentality . . . the most potent weapon in the hands of the oppressor is the mind of the oppressed. The black man is enslaved by his own thinking and attitudes more effectively than by his enslavement to any power outside himself.[15]

Black Consciousness is calling, not for a hatred of whites, but for a discovery and affirmation of black identity and unless this is understood much of the more emotive language will be misunderstood.

Black theologians have repeatedly emphasised that Black Theology is not a new theology, but a proclamation of the Gospel in such a way that it is relevant to the needs of black people in their context of humiliation and oppression. In reply to the question 'Why a *Black* Theology?', Simon Gqubule writes:

> Christ needs me as an individual with all the collected experiences I have met as a Black man, and he speaks to my situation. Therefore, Black Theology is that discipline which deals with the collected experiences of the Black man in his encounter with Christ and the world around him.[16]

Moreover, as was pointed out by E Mgojo:

> Because the word *black* has been given such a negative connotation there is a further assumption that Black Theology cannot be good theology. Interestingly enough, our interrogators do not question the legitimacy of British, German, American and Afrikaner theologies as valid expressions of Christian theology although they are identified with specific *cultures* and national identities.[17]

Black theologians have, however, not limited themselves to an affirmation of blackness, but have also explicitly criticised racism. The South Africans have re-iterated the strong repudiation of racial prejudice and discrimination which is found in the Black theology of the USA.[18] Allan Boesak, for example, has written of the threat which racism poses for the individual as well as for the church:

> Vir die swartmens is rassisme die grootste kwaad, die grootste bedreiging vir sy menswees. Dit is nog gevaarliker omdat rassisme in ons situasie deur Christene beoefen word. Swart teologie wil rassisme aansien vir wat dit is: sonde, rebellie teen God en sy evangelie, en 'n bedreiging vir die voortbestaan van sy kerk.[19]

Manas Buthelezi has asked the church this pertinent question:

Is it not true that many church buildings are no longer houses for worshipping God, the Father of Jesus Christ, but have become heathen shrines of a race and colour god?[20]

It may be asked, what is the role of the black Christian in the light of the above discussion? Negatively, he must reject all forms of racism, whether in society or in the church and he must refuse to despise himself or others. But there is also a positive role that he, or she, must play, which was outlined by Buthelezi in six theses presented at the South African Congress on Mission and Evangelism in 1973. He emphasised that the Gospel must be preached in such a way that it is relevant to the blacks whom the church seeks to address. He also stressed that the voice of black Christians should be heard, and not ignored or suppressed. Moreover, he accused whites of sabotaging and eroding the power of Christian love and of rejecting the black man as a brother. These attitudes and actions would not win blacks to the Christian faith. He said that 'for the sake of the survival of the Christian faith' the black man should step into this situation. According to him, the black man:

> . . . should now cease playing the passive role of the white man's victim. It is now time for the black man to evangelise and humanise the white man. The realisation of this will not depend on the white man's approval but solely on the black man's love for the white man.[21]

His discussion of the role that the black man is to play should not be misunderstood. It is not a simple case of an integrated or joint effort to undo the wrongs of the South African situation and work together towards a solution. Blacks are particularly suspicious of the notion of integration, because integration, in the past, has been on the white man's terms, according to the white man's analysis (and solution) to the problems of the black man.[22] Moreover, as Steve Biko pointed out in his rejection of 'white liberalism', such an integration merely encouraged the formation of a small elite who became increasingly alienated from the masses and who were unable to achieve anything for them.[23]

In their repudiation of a false integration, black theologians have been influenced by Black Consciousness, but they have not gone on to preach a new form of separatism. Sam Buti, for example,

> . . . declared himself in favour of Black Consciousness insofar as it teaches blacks to accept themselves and not set whites as their standard. 'But I hate the concept as soon as it preaches separatism,' he said. 'I cannot differentiate between Apartheid as practised in South Africa and separatism as propagated by some of the exponents of Black Consciousness.'[24]

This statement is very significant, because it indicates the extremely difficult position in which black theologians find themselves. On the one hand they are criticised by black radicals for being collaborators, and on the other they are accused by white conservatives of selling the Gospel out to black solidarity. White Christians should be conscious of the difficult position of black theologians before they speak glibly of reconciliation or integration.

White Christians should also consider what integration in the church would mean. Certainly, it would mean one and not four Dutch Reformed Churches, and in all the churches, black and white ministers with equal standing, training and salaries; mixed congregations and, therefore, a willingness to adapt and co-operate in terms of language, structure and the content of worship services. In fact, is it not this very combination of repentance, true reconciliation and joint ministry that black Christians have long asked for and *repeatedly been denied?*

Black Theology, Black Nationalism and Reconciliation

In attempting to answer the question whether black solidarity amounts to black nationalism, one needs to be aware of some diversity of opinion amongst black theologians. At times, Black Consciousness and Theology may tend towards complete fusion, as illustrated in a statement by N Pityana:

> It must be accepted then that a study of Black Theology is a study of black consciousness or self-awareness.[25]

This view is, however, the exception rather than the rule. An important difference between South African and North American Black Theology becomes evident at this very point. For example, in *The Black Messiah* (1969), Albert Cleage, a black American pastor, argued that Jesus was a black Messiah who was born into the black nation of Israel. He saw the task of Christ today as liberating the black people of America and the world. The only true interpretation of the Bible was to see it in racial terms — as a book for the liberation of blacks from white oppression. Clearly Cleage (as well as Cone) preaches a form of exclusivism and black nationalism which is *not* found amongst the vast majority of South African black theologians. In fact, Boesak has specifically repudiated any notion of black nationalism. Referring to Albert Cleage, he says:

> We fear that Cleage's Black Christian Nationalism, however well intended, cannot

and will not escape the fate of all quasi-religious nationalism. His ethic 'for the nation only' is disturbingly reminiscent of the 'for the volk only' theology black South Africans must needs reject. In Cleage's theology there is no critical distance between the Gospel and the ideology of the Black Nation, between the will of God and the desires of the nation.[27]

M Buthelezi has similarly spoken of the importance of a theology which speaks directly, and with decisiveness, to the black man, warning that:

> To interpret the quest for a Black Theology purely in terms of the awakening of black nationalism or the consolidation of Black Power forces us to trifle with one of the most fundamental issues in modern Christianity.[28]

It must not be forgotten that this repudiation by black South African theologians of black nationalism takes place against the background of Afrikaner nationalism. They reject both black nationalism and Afrikaner nationalism or so-called 'Christian Nationalism', both being regarded as alien to a Christian ethic and as dangerous forms of civil religion.[29] In the light of this, whites must realise that it is simply hypocritical to criticise blacks for seeking to affirm black identity, if they themselves are committed to the continuation of their own racial or cultural identity.

Black Theology seeks to apply the Gospel to the situation of blacks in South Africa. As such, it seeks to invalidate the claim of some white Christians that their theology is pure and unadulterated. It points out the extent to which this theology is a form of civil religion, while seeking not to fall into the same trap themselves.[30] However, although Black Theology is not identical to black nationalism, the meaning and extent of black solidarity and its interrelationship with Black Theology has not been sufficiently clarified. Given the pressure on black theologians from both black and white audiences, the distinction between theology and ideology is not a simple matter, but it cannot be avoided if Black Theology wishes to escape falling into the impasse in which much of South African theology is presently sunk. If Black Theology becomes black solidarity in theological garb, it will lead to an implicit theological affirmation of black aspirations, and to a blurring of the lines between the church and society. If this occurs, the message and the ministry of the Church will become indistinguishable from any other social agency, unable to offer hope of repentence, forgiveness and meaningful change.

It would be wrong to assume from the above that blacks have created an unbridgeable gulf between themselves and whites, or that they refuse to relate on any common basis. The fact is that black theologians still speak of the need for reconciliation, although they carefully qualify what they mean by this term. They emphatically reject what could be termed 'white tokenism', which is 'the habit of many white South Africans of trying to impress blacks by a condescending friendliness and benevolence towards them.'[31] Ernest Baartman, for instance, rejects a false or 'cheap' reconciliation that does not take into account the real issues of racism and discrimination, and that thinks blacks will be swayed by arguments that ignore these grievances. He also speaks of the 'reconciling hypocrite', ie the person who is arrogant, fearful of revealing anything of himself, suspicious of other people and in whose life Jesus Christ is not of central importance. Such a person preaches reconciliation, but practices deception and discrimination. If Christians are to be agents of reconciliation they cannot conform to this model, but must rather follow the example of Christ.[32]

Blacks are also conscious of the reality of white fear and insecurity, but as Buthelezi points out: 'Without reconciliation there can never be any security.'[33] His point is twofold: the theological basis for security is Christ's atoning work which makes reconciliation between man and God possible. But reconciliation must go further, and draw together the threatened, and the threatening, in South Africa. He then goes on to say that the attempt to invest whites with a feeling of security by means of a rigid separation has failed. It is at this point that Black Theology seeks to take up the prophetic and reconciling mission of the Church, so that people in South Africa can enter into the liberating security of the Gospel.[34]. It must be noted that black theologians in South Africa, unlike many in the USA, speak not only of the mutual respect that must precede and accompany the work of reconciliation, but also of the love that the two groups must have for each other. Ernest Baartman addressed his fellow blacks in 1973 as follows:

> You must so love the white man that he must see it as his Christian calling to share power with you. You must so love the white man that you become a Thou rather than an It. You must so love him for his sake, for his humanity, you will never allow him to treat you as an It.[35]

Finally, reconciliation between black and white, it is clearly stated, cannot be seen to be valid or meaningful unless it is accompanied by a change in the life circumstances of black people. Reconciliation and oppression cannot exist simultaneously. Boesak stresses that whites must realise that mere talk about reconciliation is empty and false. Oppression and reconciliation are mutually exclusive. While the white man is an oppressor how can he also be a brother?[36]

It can be seen that Black Consciousness, especially the form in which it is advocated by Black Theology, is extremely significant for South African society and the Church. Black Theology deals with the vital issues of racism, black identity, integration, nationalism and reconciliation, and if the Church ignores this message, it does so at the risk of compromising its identity and destroying its unity.

The understanding of Black Theology regarding Black Consciousness is not, however, centred purely on an acknowledgement of black identity and a repudiation of racism at a personal level. On the contrary, Black Theology has sought to address itself to the total situation of blacks in South Africa and, therefore, to both interpersonal relationships and societal structures. Black Consciousness is born within a context of unjust structures, and leads inevitably to an analysis of them. It is, therefore, to a consideration of Black Theology as Liberation Theology that this discussion must now turn.

Notes

1 Steve Biko, *I write what I like* (London: Heinemann, 1978) p49. In fact, because of the relatively small number of Indian Christians, most of the next two chapters deal with the writings of black Africans. Even within the Coloured community, Boesak is virtually the only well-known Christian spokesman.

2 It could be argued that Black Theology has its roots in the Congo of 1700, when a young Congolese girl, Beatrice, preached, amongst other things, that Christ and all his apostles were black and that Christ identified with suffering Africans and not with the oppressive whites. Cf D Bosch, 'Currents and Crosscurrents in South African Black Theology' in GS Wilmore and JH Cone, *A Documentary History of Black Theology: 1966—1979*, p220.

3 See Gail Gerhart, *Black Power in South Africa: The Evolution of an Ideology* and Edward Roux, *Time Longer than Rope: The Black Man's Struggle for Freedom in South Africa* (University of Wisconsin Press, 1948/1964). Whereas these two books are more concerned with black political events and developments, there are others that deal more specifically with the Church's involvement in, and reaction to, the South African context. Besides those that I have already referred to, there is also the more recent *The South African Churches in a Revolutionary Situation* (Maryknoll, New York: Orbis, 1981) by Marjorie Hope and James Young. This book provides a useful and readable survey, but lacks the necessary detailed analysis.

4 JW de Gruchy, *The Church Struggle in South Africa*, p152.

5 This would seem to be the position taken by Professor Carel Boshoff (former Chairman of the Broederbond and Head of the Theology Faculty at the University of Pretoria). See his book *Swart Teologie: van Amerika tot in Suid-Afrika* (Pretoria: NG Boekhandel, 1980), and article 'Christ in Black Theology in a South African Context' (Paper read at the SA Missiological Society Annual Congress, Potchefstroom, 1981) pp1—20. Incidentally, this paper evoked a storm of protest and disagreement from the majority of the delegates present at the Congress.

6 Gail Gerhart, *Black Power in South Africa*, p273.

7 JW de Gruchy gives 1966 for the establishment of UCM (*The Church Struggle in South Africa*, p154).

8 For further information see JW de Gruchy *The Church Struggle in South Africa* p154ff and the South African Institute of Race Relations (SAIRR) 1967 and 1968

yearbooks.

9 The papers at this conference, with some additions, were first published by UCM and edited by Sabelo Ntwasa. When Ntwasa was placed under a banning order, Ravan Press published *Essays in Black Theology* edited by M Mothlabi (1972). This book was then banned in its year of publication. Two overseas editions are presently available: *Black Theology: The South African Voice* (London: C Hurst, 1973) and B Moore (ed), *The Challenge of Black Theology in South Africa* (Atlanta, Georgia: John Knox Press, 1974).

10 These were 'The Christian Challenge and Black Theology' by M Buthelezi and 'Black Consciousnss and the Black Church' by James Cone. See T Thoahlane (ed), *Black Renaissance* (Johannesburg: Ravan Press, 1975).

11 See M Buthelezi, 'Change in the Church' *SAO* (August 1973) p129.

12 E Baartman, 'The Significance of the Development of Black Consciousness for the Church' *JTSA* 2 (1973) pp18—19.

13 M Buthelezi, 'The Christian Presence in Today's South Africa' *JTSA* 16 (1976) p7.

14 A Small, 'Blackness versus Nihilism: Black Racism Rejected' in B Moore (ed), *The Challenge of Black Theology in South Africa*, p11ff.

15 D Bosch, 'Currents and Crosscurrents in South African Black Theology' in Gayraud S Wilmore and James H Cone (eds), *Black Theology: A Documentary History, 1966—1979*, p230. See also G Gerhart's discussion of Franz Fanon in her book *Black Power in South Africa*, pp14ff, 274ff and 281ff.

16 S Gqubule, 'What is Black Theology?' *JTSA* 8 (1974) p19.

17 E Mgojo, 'Prolegomenon to the Study of Black Theology' *JTSA* 21 (1977) p27.

18 See the statements on racism by the NCBC (National Conference of Black Churchmen), and James Cone in GS Wilmore and JH Cone (eds), *Black Theology: A Documentary History, 1966—1979*, pp 101 and 120. In fact, it is in the Black Theology of the USA and South Africa that the emphasis on *black* liberation introduced the issue of racial analysis to the predominantly *class* analysis of Latin American liberation theologies.

19 A Boesak, 'Waarheen wil Swart Teologie?' *Pro V* (February, 1974) p5.

20 M Buthelezi, 'Christianity in SA' *Pro V* (15 June, 1973) p4. For some white views on this point see the document *Human Relations in the South African Scene in the Light of Scripture* (the official DRC view). For a critique of the latter see B Johanson, 'Race, Mission and Ecumenism: Reflections on the Landman Report' *JTSA* 10 (1975) pp51—61 and D Bax, *A Different Gospel: A Critique of the Theology behind Apartheid*, (Johannesburg: The Presbyterian Church of SA, 1979?)

21 M Buthelezi, 'Six Theses: Theological Problems of Evangelism in the South African Context' *JTSA* 3 (1973) pp55—56.

22 D Bosch, 'The Case for Black Theology' *Pro V* (15 August, 1972) pp1 and 2.

23 S Biko, *I write what I like,* p19ff.

24 Sam Buti, *Ecunews* (17 June, 1975), quoted by E Regehr, *Perceptions of Apartheid: The Churches and Political Change in South Africa,* (Kitchener, Ontario: Between the Lines, 1979) p226.

25 N Pityana, 'What is Black Consciousness?' in B Moore (ed), *The Challenge of Black Theology in South Africa,* p58.

26 A Cleage, *The Black Messiah* (New York: Sheed and Ward, 1969).

27 A Boesak, 'Civil Religion and the Black Community', *JTSA* 19 (1977) p43.

28 M Buthelezi, 'An African Theology or a Black Theology?' in B Moore (ed), *The Challenge of Black Theology in South Africa,* p29.

29 See A Boesak's *Farewell to Innocence* pp88—92.

30 For a discussion of the extent to which Black Theology has been successful in this attempt, cf H Pretorius 'Wit/Swart Bevrydingsteologie in Suid- Afrika' *NGTT* 18:4 (1977) 343—352.

31 D Bosch, 'Currents and Crosscurrents in South African Black Theology' in GS Wilmore and JH Cone (eds), *Black Theology: A Documentary History, 1966—1979*, p230.

32 E Baartman, 'The Reconciling Hypocrite' (unpublished paper read at the Consultation of the ASATI Staff Institute, Rosettenville, 16 January, 1975) pp6—17. A similar point is made by the white theologian, Adrio König, in 'Die Roeping van die Kerk in die Heersende Politieke en Ekonomiese Probleme in Suid-Afrika' *T Via* 6:1 (July, 1978) pp43—53.

33 M Buthelezi, 'The Relevance of Black Theology' *SAO* (December, 1974) p199.

34 M Buthelezi, *ibid*.

35 E Baartman, 'The Signifiance of the Development of Black Consciousness for the Church' *JTSA* 2 (1973) p20. The significance of the date of this article must not be missed, for, as will be shown in the following chapter, the frustration and anger of blacks has increased and this has, in some cases, changed the tone of their writings.

36 A Boesak, 'Swart Bewussyn, Swart Mag en "Kleurling Politiek" ' (Black Consciousness, Black Power and "Coloured Politics"), *Pro V* (February, 1977) p9ff.

CHAPTER SIX

Black Liberation and Black Theology

South African Black Theology, because of its great concern for liberation, can accurately be described as a Liberation Theology, and is regarded as such by several of its proponents. Desmond Tutu, for example, says: 'I count Black Theology in the category of liberation theologies.'[1] Such a statement, however, raises the question of the relationship between South African Black Theology and other theologies of liberation.

It would appear that black theologians in South Africa, while they often use the term 'liberation', were not, initially, *directly* influenced by the Latin American liberation theologians. This is clear from the fact that there are very few references to the primary thinkers in Latin America, and also from a lack of contact between the South African and Latin American theologians at conferences, especially during the earlier years of the development of South African Black Theology.[2] As de Gruchy points out, there are also significant differences between the two:

> These differences are evident especially in ecclesiology, that is, the study of the nature and task of the church, and on the issue of the relationship between Christian faith and ideology, notably Marxism . . . Black theologians in South Africa . . . have never advocated any ideological alliance with Marxism.[3]

However, while South African Black Theology does not share the Latin American emphasis on a Marxist analysis of society, it does share its stress on the importance of the situation from within which, and to which, theology must speak.

James Cone provided the major outside influence on South African black theology in the development of its liberation emphasis. According to him:

> The significance of Black Theology lies in the conviction that the content of the

Christian gospel is liberation, so that any talk about God that fails to take seriously the righteousness of God as revealed in the liberation of the weak and
downtrodden is not Christian language. . . . To speak of the God of Christianity
is to speak of him who has defined himself according to the liberation of the oppressed.[4]

This theme was taken up and strongly expressed in the subsequent publication
of *Essays in Black Theology* and recurs repeatedly in the writings of many
black theologians. As Basil Moore put it: 'Black Theology . . . is a theology of
the oppressed, by the oppressed, for the liberation of the oppressed.'[5] This emphasis on liberation is also found in the earliest book on South African Black
Theology namely, Boesak's *Farewell to Innocence*, where Cone's central thesis
is clearly reflected in the statement that Black Theology,

> . . . believes that liberation is not only 'part of' the gospel, or 'consistent with' the
> gospel, it is the content and framework of the gospel of Jesus Christ.[6]

As was stated in the previous chapter, however, it is not valid to argue that
Cone's liberationist emphasis was simply imposed on South Africa. Its
espousal by black theologians is a consequence of their conviction that it is
pertinent to their context and their desire for liberation. This is seen in
Boesak's statement that:

> Black Theology, therefore, because it comes from a situation of oppression and
> suffering of a people who believe in God and who ask what the Gospel of Jesus
> Christ has to say about the situation, is also a theology of liberation.[7]

As will be shown later, it is also open to question whether the South African
black theologians' espousal of Cone's thinking is entirely uncritical.

In order to facilitate the reader's understanding of this aspect of South
African Black Theology I have divided this chapter into four sections. The first
deals with the hermeneutics of liberation theology, the second with the meaning of terms such as 'liberation' and 'the poor', while the third concentrates on
the Church. The last section consists of a few critical comments.

What is 'Hermeneutics'?

The term hermeneutics basically means interpretation. Thus, we may speak of
biblical hermeneutics, which simply means the way in which the Bible is interpreted by its readers.

Much work has been done in recent years on this question of the nature of
hermeneutics, bringing several factors into sharper focus.[8] The most impor-

tant of these is that no-one can glibly claim to 'just believe what the Bible says'. This is because, as a result of our education, background, church context, etc, we read the Bible, albeit unconsciously, through a certain set of spectacles. For this reason many theologians are strongly critical of some 'traditional' understandings of Biblical interpretation. They argue that it is both simplistic and false, to think that all we need to do is understand the Bible and then apply it to our situation, as represented thus:

In a very readable article, René Padilla (a Latin American theologian) has criticised models such as these, arguing that the message of the Bible is, because of the nature of revelation, embodied within a cultural context. If this context is misunderstood, or regarded as normative, misinterpretation of the text will inevitably result. Not only is this so, but the interpreter, in his or her interpretation of the meaning of the Biblical text for today, is also viewing it from within a particular context or culture, viz:

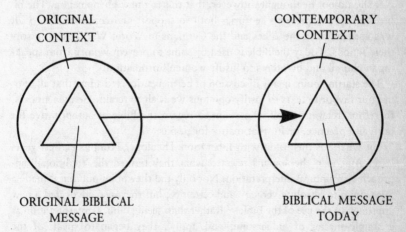

Padilla outlines three common approaches to biblical interpretation, the 'intuitive', 'scientific' and 'contextual'. The 'intuitive' stresses an immediate apprehension and personal application of the Bible. This approach is often found in, for example, older commentaries and devotional literature. The 'scientific' on the other hand, emphasises the 'tools' of biblical criticism, anthropology, linguistics and the like. This approach is valuable in as far as it seeks to interpret correctly the biblical cultures, but it fails to sufficiently recognise the influence of the reader's context on what he/she sees or concludes from the Bible. The 'contextual', however, while it does not reject the other two, points out that the role of *both* the ancient *and* modern cultures and world-views and their effect on revelation cannot be ignored. Both profoundly influence the way in which the biblical texts are recorded and understood.[10]

'Contextual' theologians have pointed out that in the very process of reading and 'understanding' the Bible we are already interpreting it in our own way. What is more, in our subsequent 'application to the situation' we are applying texts that we have *selected*, to a situation which we have *interpreted*, according to our own viewpoint.

This can, for example, be illustrated by referring to the on-going disagreement between the so-called English liberal churches and white Afrikaner churches in South Africa. Many of the former read the Bible assiduously and find that apartheid is a heresy, that it cannot be justified theologically and that it is evil. Many of the latter read the Bible equally assiduously and decide that separate development is God's own solution to the complex problems of race relations in South Africa.

Why is this so? Simply because each group approaches the Bible with preconceived notions, and then inevitably finds in it justification for the beliefs it already holds.

It should not be thought, however, that this is a new phenomenon. The Bible was used in previous centuries both to support and condemn slavery. It was used by both the Allies and the Germans in World War Two to justify their actions. Today the Bible is used by some to prevent women from speaking in church and by others to justify women's ordination!

The starting point in any discussion of hermeneutics is to admit that all of us use our favourite texts to justify opinions we wish to retain. Hermeneutics is, therefore, relevant to all who claim to regard the Bible as authoritative for faith and practice, or for that matter for praxis.

But what has this to do with Liberation Theology? From its earliest years Latin American theologians rejected what they termed the 'traditional' approach to scriptural interpretation. Not only did they point out that it made a false claim to absolute veracity and certainty, but they also advocated a new approach to the use of the Bible.[11] Rather than seeing biblical interpretation as a simple matter of 'understand and apply', they began to speak of the hermeneutical circle. In this model, one begins with the situation, moves around to the Bible and then back to the situation.

THE HERMENEUTICAL CIRCLE

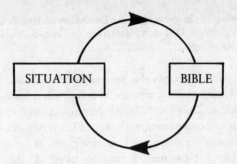

Liberation theologians also speak of a hermeneutical *key* — which will unlock the meaning of the Bible. This key is *liberation*. To put it another way, the Bible's teaching on liberation is the touchstone and foundation of biblical interpretation.

With these preliminary remarks in mind, let us now examine the hermeneutical principles employed in South African Black Theology.

It would not be inaccurate to say that Black Theology is first and foremost a situational theology. In other words, it deliberately seeks to relate the Christian faith to the life situation of the black person in South Africa.[12] This interest is clearly reflected in the 1971 SASO Commission on Black Theology which stated that:

> Black Theology is not a theology of absolutes but grapples with existential situations. Black Theology is not a theology of theory but that of action and development. It is not a reaction against anything but it is an authentic and positive articulation of the Black Christian's reflection on God in the light of black experience.[13]

Black Theology, therefore, begins its theological reflection within the framework of its understanding of the situation of blacks in South Africa. Then, on the basis of this understanding, it calls for a liberation of the poor and oppressed. It is thus the exploitative situation and the need for liberation that is the starting point for their theological reflection.

The need for liberation is also the context to which this theological reflection must speak. Any theology which refuses to take account of this situation is regarded as being bound to the world-view and interests of the oppressors.[14] Thus, for Boesak, Liberation Theology is a new proclamation of the 'age-old gospel'. It is a proclamation that is freed from 'the deadly hold of the mighty and the powerful' and it correctly perceives the liberating message of the Bible. He puts it like this:

> Liberation Theology, by beginning with the Exodus, by making theology a critical reflection on the praxis of liberation places the gospel in its authentic perspective, namely that of liberation . . .[15]

In this way Black Theology accepts liberation as its hermeneutical key, the key that unlocks the meaning of the Scriptures. In doing this, it has combined the situational emphasis of Cone (ie the belief that blacks need to be liberated from their situation of exploitation), with that of Latin American Liberation Theology (which regards the primacy of liberation praxis as the solution to the hermeneutical problem). How then, it may be asked, do they justify this hermeneutical approach?

Although black theologians in South Africa have not discussed the validity of theological reflection 'in the light of the black situation' in any detail, it must not be assumed that they are entirely unaware of the difficulties and dangers of such a hermeneutical procedure. Boesak has, for example, qualified the use of 'the situation' in Black Theology and questioned Cone's usage of black experience as the determining factor of biblical interpretation:

> The black situation is the situation within which reflection and action take place, but it is the World[sic] of God which illuminates the reflection and guides the action. We fear that Cone attaches too much theological import to the black experience and the black situation as if these realities *within themselves* have revelational value on a par with Scripture. God, it seems to us, reveals himself *in* the situation, the Word is being heard in the situation, thereby giving meaning to the situation. The black experience provides the framework within which blacks understand the revelation of God in Jesus Christ. No more no less.[16]

B Goba, while he admits that Black Theology is committed to the black communal praxis (by which he means the situation which black people share), argues that it should not absolutise this communal praxis. Or, to put it differently, black experience should not become the only standard by which to judge the validity of theological thinking. He also speaks of the need for 'a hermeneutical praxis', ie 'a theological interpretation of meaning informed by the scriptures and our experience and geared to active involvement in the liberation process'.[17] Goba appears to be convinced of the primacy of the social context but does not explain in this article how the black theological hermeneutic can remain both authoritative and relevant, if it is ultimately governed by an ever-changing situation.

Similarly, in a discussion of the use of Scripture in Black Theology, EK Mosothoane says that 'it seems quite clear that liberation represents black theology's "hermeneutical key" '.[18] He claims, however, that this does *not* amount to an attempt to produce proof texts to prove a particular point, but rather is a way of stressing those texts which 'illuminate' the Bible for us. He admits however, that:

> . . . the possibility of forcing onto some individual texts of Scripture, in the process of explicating the liberation theme in the Bible, meanings they do not in fact carry, must be recognised.[19]

Having made this qualification, Mosothoane then indicates that he accepts, with some qualifications, that for Black Theology, liberation is a hermeneutical key, for he concludes that:

> Black Theology approached Scripture with a heavy burden of oppression, rejection and suffering, seeking to discover in Scripture God's purpose for humanity in situations of that nature. It understands the divine purpose essentially and fundamentally in terms of liberation . . .[20]

S Dwane offers another way of seeking to grapple with the difficulty of relating theological reflection to a black context. In defending Liberation Theology against criticism, he has maintained that the emphasis of Liberation is an *aspect* of black theological thought. As he puts it:

> To refer to a particular emphasis in the theological discipline as liberation theology is not an attempt by the part to usurp what belongs to the whole, but rather an endeavour to sharpen the idea of liberation as a legitimate aspect of the theological debate as a whole.[21]

It is important to note that, in saying this, he is differing from the perspective held by Boesak. It is one thing to see liberation theology as an aspect of the Gospel and an attempt to emphasise God's concern for the oppressed (as Dwane goes on to argue), and quite another to say, as Boesak does, that the Gospel *is* liberation.

Finally, mention must be made of E Mgojo's criticism of James Cone's interpretation of the Bible. He contrasts Cone's *Black Theology and Black Power* with his second book, *A Black Theology for Liberation*.[22] The former he classifies as 'Christian sociology' because of its primary emphasis on black experience and, regarding the latter, he goes on to argue that:

> . . . by shifting his major premise from the black condition to the Gospel of Jesus Christ (ie the Christian faith), Cone is indeed engaging in Christian Theology.[23]

It may be questioned, however, whether Cone has indeed shifted his starting point as much as Mgojo seems to imply, since the need for black liberation from a situation of oppression is both the starting point and the goal of all Cone's theology.

Mgojo also discusses the use of the 'sources' of Black Theology, ie Biblical revelation, experience, black history, culture and tradition.[24] He prefers to call these sources 'formative factors' because they cannot be drawn upon without qualification. He also asserts that they must not be accorded normative status. Biblical revelation, he argues, is the most important of these 'formative factors' and Black Theology, in order to be valid and authoritative, must rest on it, and not on the thought or activities of black theologians. Thus he warns:

> One can become so engrossed with the question related to black experience as to forget that theology must always glorify God and clarify what he had done.[25]

It would appear from the above that Boesak, Goba and Mosothoane all agree that liberation must be regarded as a hermeneutical key, although they do also seek to guard against ideological manipulation of the text on the basis of the concerns of black experience. Moreover, they would all reject the 'traditional' assumption (which some people still hold to) that theology can be done in a fully objective manner, ie without being either conditioned or influenced by one's social and intellectual context. They claim that a truer representation would be that of the hermeneutical circle. For these three theologians, the starting point is their social context, ie the condition of oppression and the desire for liberation. From this point, theological reflection moves around the 'hermeneutical circle' to the Bible, is informed by it, and continues around, back to the situation.

Although it is not clear whether Dwane would accept the above understanding of liberation as a hermeneutical key, he does accept the importance both of the situation of the oppressed and the need for a Liberation Theology which he believes can 'bring black and white Christians to the cross where they can come face to face with themselves, with God and with each other . . .'[26] Liberation Theology can also break the ideological stranglehold that apartheid has on theology.

Mgojo, on the other hand, while he accepts black experience as an essential correlate to biblical revelation, seeks to argue that it is the latter that must be the authoritative norm.[27] At first glance this position seems clear, but once it is examined more closely, it does appear to be vulnerable to the same criticism as that of Boesak's. This is because Mgojo himself seems to be part of a hermeneutical circle within which he seeks to give priority of place to the Bible as the necessary starting point. However, he also quotes, with approval, a statement by D Roberts that 'Experience determines the need, the meaning and the effectiveness of revelation in the human situation.'[28] It would appear that in this article Mgojo is not altogether clear as to the precise role of black experience in biblical interpretation.

As can be gathered from the above descriptions and analyses, South African black theologians have given some attention to the matter of hermeneutics. On the one hand, they emphasis that theology must not be an abstract exercise, but relate to the concrete realities of human, and especially black, existence. On the other hand, they have sought to avoid the pitfall of reducing theology to ideology and thereby distorting it in the cause of black liberation. To what extent they have succeeded in this self-imposed task only time will tell. It also remains to be seen how the black liberation theologians of the 1980s will deal with these issues.

The Meaning of Liberation and the Identity of the Poor

One of the earliest definitions of liberation from within Black Theology is A Mpunzi's.[29] He speaks of the 'two faces of freedom' which, though inter-related, can be distinguished. Firstly, there is the attitudinal aspect, which is the freedom of blacks to be able to affirm themselves *as blacks* rather than denying this identity and thereby negating their very humanity. This formulation is very similar to M Buthelezi's view of the liberation of the human spirit:

> Many people have understood liberation as only referring to physical and political domination. I contend that liberation has also something to do with the liberation of the spirit . . . When the black man begins to create concepts about his life, destiny and aspirations, that would be part of the process of liberation.[30]

This attitudinal aspect was discussed in the previous chapter.

The second of Mpunzi's 'two faces of freedom' is the structural aspect. This is the individual's freedom, in that his uniqueness is accepted by the community, and he is allowed to make his contribution towards that community's continued existence. This structural aspect is the major concern of Liberation Theology. Lest it be thought to be an exclusive concern, however, it is necessary to heed Boesak's statement that Black Theology:

> . . . focuses on the dependency of the oppressed and their liberation from dependency in all its dimensions — psychological, cultural, political, economic and theological. It expresses the belief that because Christ's liberation has come, the total liberation of man can no longer be denied.[31]

An important part of the understanding of liberation, especially in Boesak's writings, is the theme of Black Power.[32] He regards Black Power as being the appropriate response to the white man's power structure, ie the system of apartheid, which has led to the degradation and exploitation of the black man. For Boesak, Black Power is a 'slogan' for the continuing historical effort of black people to achieve justice by forcing whites to change the existing structures. He does *not* regard Black Power as synonymous with the Gospel, but does emphasise that Black Theology is seeking to respond to the South African situation by stressing the need for liberation *from* injustice and *towards* 'the mobilisation of black people for participation *with power* in the public arenas of policy decision-making'.[33]

Other black theologians, like Buthelezi and Baartman, have been critical of the notion of Black Power but when their remarks are considered carefully it is evident that they are using this term in a different sense to that of Boesak. By Black Power, they mean black nationalism, which they reject. However, they do *not* reject the concept of blacks exercising responsibility and living out their God-given task of stewardship over the earth or, in the South African context, of power-sharing.[34]

In concentrating on the hope of liberation, two biblical texts are given priority of place. These are the Exodus narrative in the OT and Jesus' quotation of Isaiah 61 in his 'sermon' in the synagogue of Nazareth (Luke 4. 18—19). Although it is primarily in the work of the Latin American thinkers that these two texts are expounded upon and regarded as normative paradigms of God's activity in the Bible (and of course in the contemporary situation), they also occur in South African Black Theology.

Liberation, thus, is understood largely in terms of black people being set free from a situation of oppression. Significantly, many black theologians, especially since the 1976 protests, are speaking not merely in terms of injustices, but are calling for a 'total' liberation of black people from exploitation.[35]

What can be said of the identity of the poor who need to be liberated? It would appear that James Cone has sought to see 'the poor' in the NT as meaning only the materially poor, and that he regards the Kingdom as belonging to the poor *alone*. Thus, his interpretation tends to exclude all but the oppressed (or those whom he regards as the oppressed) from the promises of the Gospel.[36] In South Africa, this view was taken up by Basil Moore who sought to argue that the message and ministry of Jesus were directed primarily, even exclusively, to the poor and the oppressed.[37]

Boesak's treatment of 'the poor' does not, however, conform to this pattern of interpretation. It is true that he rejects attempts to 'spiritualise' passages such as Luke 4. 18—19, and emphasises that:

. . . the *poor* Jesus was speaking of can only be understood as those who are materially poor in the first place, in other words, those who die of hunger, who are illiterate, who are exploited by others.[38]

Unlike Cone, however, Boesak does not reject the 'poor in spirit' (Matt 5.3) in favour of 'the poor' (Luke 6.20), but rather seeks to retain the meaning of both terms and, in support of this interpretation, he quotes HN Ridderbos's statement that:

These 'poor' or 'poor in spirit' (the meek) appear again and again in the Old Testament, particularly in the Psalms and in the Prophets. They represent the socially oppressed, those who suffer from the power of injustice and are harassed by those who only consider their own advantages and influence. They are, however, at the same time those who remain faithful to God and expect their salvation from his Kingdom alone.[39]

EK Mosothoane concurs with an interpretation of 'the poor' as the materially poor, but, in analysing Matt 11. 5—6, he goes on to discuss the *hamartōloi, pornai* and *telōnai* and points out that these were the sinners and outcasts, the disreputable people of Jesus' society and the ones on whom he had compassion.[40] He stresses that Christians, if they are truly Jesus' disciples, cannot turn their eyes away from these generally despised people. Mosothoane not only broadens the understanding of the identity of 'the poor', but also goes on to warn African Christians:

Do not think that just because you are an African all is well with you. Do not conclude that your black skin automatically puts you on God's side.[41]

Similarly, in 1972, Bishop Alphaeus Zulu said that a careless use of the term 'the oppressed' could lead to misinterpretation and misuse:

Black theologians, however, need to guard against equating 'God being on the side of the oppressed' with 'the oppressed being on the side of God'.[42]

This warning was repeated at the Pan-Africanist Conference of Third World Theologians (Accra, 1977) when Bishop Tutu said:

Oppressed peoples must hear that, according to the Bible, this God is always on the side of the downtrodden. He is so graciously on their side not because they are more virtuous and better than their oppressors, but solely and simply because they are oppressed, he is that kind of a God . . . those whom God has saved must become the servants of others, for they are saved ultimately not for their self-aggrandisement or self-glorification, but so that they may bring others to a saving knowledge of God.[43]

From all these views, it would seem that black South African theologians have shown remarkable restraint, in resisting the temptation to preach a liberation which excludes whites and fails to challenge or criticise blacks.

Liberation Theology and the Church

This discussion of Liberation Theology would not be complete unless its implications for the Church were also mentioned. This is because liberation theologians have specifically directed a great deal of attention to the church and the role which it plays in society.

In their discussion of the inter-relation between liberation and the Church, black theologians have concentrated on two basic issues. The *first* consists of criticising both the 'pietist' and 'collaborationist' models.[44] The 'pietists' are represented, generally speaking, by the English churches and the 'collaborationists' by the Afrikaans-speaking churches. *The second issue* to which black theologians have directed themselves is understanding the nature and the role of the Church.

The 'pietists' are criticised on the grounds that their 'spiritualised' theology and belief in saving 'souls' has prevented them from being aware of, and becoming actively concerned about, the needs of the whole person. They have ignored or rejected the socio-political content of the Gospel.[45] Manas Buthelezi says:

> To my mind the ulimate criterion for the spread of Christianity is not just how many people go to church on a Sunday, but how many people allow that which is unique in the Christian Gospel to share their lives as well as the spirit of their social, economic and political environment.[46]

The English-speaking churches, many of which have large black memberships, are further censured because of the fact that so much of their leadership is concentrated in the hands of the whites. This means that the voice of black Christians is not sufficiently clearly heard or acted upon in the churches.[47] Even if certain important leaders (eg in the Methodist Church) are black, the vast majority of the leaders are white. Also, many white congregations pay little heed to the decisions of top leadership regarding the role of the church in socio-political affairs. In addition, the continuing lack of fellowship is largely responsible for perpetuating the ignorance and mistrust that exist between Christians of various racial groups. Both Buthelezi and Gqubule strongly emphasise the need for *meaningful* contact at both leadership and local church fellowship levels.[48]

The Afrikaans churches, on the other hand, are criticised for their ideological captivity, in the sense that they have not differentiated themselves from their *volk*, failing to be sufficiently critical of its political ideology and permitting the development of a pseudo-religious ideology of nationalism in their churches.[49] S Gqubule has described such churches as being in bondage to the assumptions of white superiority, bound to cultural and national norms that are actually in conflict with the Gospel.[50] Particular attention has been paid to the racial and ethnic divisions which encourage and perpetuate differences rather than seeking to work for church unity.[51]

Over the past decade, relations between the so-called 'mother church' (Nederduitse Gereformeerde Kerk) and the 'daughter' churches (Nederduitse Gereformeerde Kerk in Afrika, Reformed Church in Africa and Sendingkerk) have steadily deteriorated. These tensions can be seen in the formation of the 'Broederkring' (a group of the more radical ministers of the three black NG churches) and the NGKA's decision to join the SACC in 1975(the NGK withdrew in 1941). But matters really came to a head at the Conference of the World Alliance of Reformed Churches in Ottawa in August 1982. In the study guide for delegates, Dr Allan Boesak wrote a devastating critique of racism as practised in the Church and especially in the white reformed Churches in South Africa.[52] This article, together with events and resolutions at the Conference, including Boesak's election as president and the exclusion of the white South African Reformed Churches, caused such a rumpus that when I returned home, after being overseas, late in September 1982, the newspapers were still reverberating from the impact.

Perhaps the most vehement condemnation, which is directed against all the white churches, has centred around the ignorance, apathy and selfishness of the white population regarding the suffering that blacks continue to experience as a result of the practical outworkings of separate development. Sam Buti, for example, in a sermon preached at Crossroads squatter camp in 1978, said:

> You dare not accept a man's sweat and labour and at the same time reject him as a person; you dare not view him purely as a labour unit and dismiss or ignore him as a human being. If you accept him as a human being, then you must accept his normal basic needs and make provision for needs such as family life, housing, transportation, medical care, recreation and education. Anything less than this is exploitation — in fact it could even become another form of slavery.[53]

Finally, what does Black Theology regard as the role of the church in South African society? As has been mentioned throughout this book, it emphasises the need for communication, real reconciliation and change *within* the church, so that it can more authentically live as the people of God. However, Black Theology also places emphasis on the role that the church must play in society as a whole. As the (white) moderator of the Sendingkerk (NGSK), D Botha, put it:

> Mere interest in mission work, in saving souls for Christ and expanding the Church, is not enough . . . To survive in our turbulent times the Church has to risk leaving its secure isolation and, in the name of Christ and his Kingdom, participate in the struggle for peace and justice, for the liberation of mankind from the powers and structures of oppression, discrimination and selfishness . . .[54]

It must not be assumed that liberation theologians believe that a change in political and economic circumstances will automatically lead to a 'golden age', for as Tutu points out:

> This is a misreading of liberation theology. Liberation Theologians have too much evidence that the removal of one oppressor means the replacement by another; yesterday's victim quite rapidly becomes today's dictator. Liberation theologians know only too well the recalcitrance of human nature and so accept the traditional doctrines of the fall and original sin, but they also know that God has provided the remedy in Jesus Christ.[55]

Some Concluding Remarks

What has been said above may seem to some to be going too far along the road of the politicisation of the Gospel, and so it would be useful to briefly discuss an article on Atonement written by Professor Simon Maimela of the University of South Africa.[56] He is critical of some of the previous understandings of atonement because of, amongst other things, their individualism, which he feels is the result of an inadequate understanding of both sin and salvation. Sin, as the Bible itself indicates, is far more than the *individual's* evil and guilt. Moreover, human sinfulness poisons not only interpersonal relationships, but also the broader social, even international, framework of life.[57] Therefore, the old (pietistic) understandings of salvation are hopelessly limited:

> Salvation becomes a sort of translation of individuals out of this unredeemed and oppressive situation into some mystic communion with God . . . [But] to reduce the entire work of Christ on the cross to the forgiveness of sins and guilt is to overlook the liberating and transformative power of Christ's work in socio-political conditions, a power which is at work to free men and women from the tyranny of racism, class, sex, poverty and ignorance.[58]

Maimela is challenging Christians to rethink the implications of the salvation which they preach, both for the Church itself and in terms of its witness and task in relation to society at large.[59] So long as the personal dimension is not pushed aside or discarded in favour of the socio-political dimension, Liberation Theology can bring a renewed vision of witness and service to the Church in South Africa.

Does all this mean that Black Theology is moving towards an unqualified affirmation of black aspirations? I believe that such a judgement would be mistaken, for certain important qualifications are made by many black theologians. As has already been shown, Black Theology has not cut itself off, entirely, from the white churches, but has rather sought to articulate what it sees as necessary reforms and changes. Moreover, many of Black Theology's criticisms, as will be shown in chapter seven, have been advanced by white theologians as well. Nor do black theologians assert their unconditional sympathy with black nationalism, and, indeed, many would specifically repudiate such an alliance. Nevertheless, Black Theology does interpret the role of the Church in terms of a struggle for liberation and, therefore, theology and the Church are viewed from within this framework. According to B Goba:

> Being the people of God within the South African context means . . . a rediscovery of our solidarity in Christ as we engage in his love and mission of liberation . . . The communal dimension of those who enjoy a deep fellowship with Christ forces them to become witnesses to the unity made possible by their participation in God's Liberation revealed in Jesus Christ. (1 John 4:19—21).[60]

Although Goba is committed to this task of liberation, he argues that the Church cannot ultimately be an 'ideological community', whether that ideology is related to a programme of separate development or to any black nationalistic or tribal aspirations.[61]

In order to prevent misunderstanding of this liberation theme in Black Theology, it must be remembered that it arises out of a context within which blacks are subjected to legislative injustice, discriminated against on the basis of their race and dispossessed of a great range of educational, political and economic rights and privileges. Moreover, they are confronted with a seemingly intransigent government and an immensely powerful system of state security, in the face of which black theologians have persisted in calling for the liberation of their people from oppression.

In their discussion of 'the poor', black theologians have, understandably, greatly stressed material poverty and political oppression. For them, passages such as Matt 25. 31—46 are not merely the subject of speculative inquiry, but speak with great force to their situation. Their concern is not limited to providing relief for the poor, but includes a desire to see structural changes that will remove the causes of poverty and starvation. In this, they seek to speak on behalf of both the Church and black people generally. This does not, however, mean that they have interpreted 'the poor' in a reductionist fashion, for they speak also of the 'poor in spirit'. They stress the responsibility of the Church of Christ to minister, as he did, to the poor. Nevertheless, it would seem to be valid to point out that a certain tension is apparent within Black Theology with regard to 'the poor' who have turned to God in their need and appropriated his salvation, and 'the poor', who are not part of the people of God. This tension is then compounded by the frequent use of language such as 'God is always on the side of the oppressed.'

Turning now to the issue of liberation hermeneutics, a few points need to be raised.

It must be said that the proponents of Liberation Theology have done theology a great service in emphasising that the ways in which the Bible is interpreted must be opened up for further examination. All theologians must acknowledge that their interpretations of the text are influenced by the assumptions and questions with which they approach the Bible. Further, liberation theologians could perhaps be said to be more honest in that they have openly admitted that they come to the Bible with questions regarding the situation of the poor and oppressed.[62]

Although Liberation Theology has certainly exposed the hermeneutical problem, some of its solutions to this problem are open to question. This is particularly true of some of the Latin American thinkers, many of whom adopt the OT Exodus narrative and Luke 4. 18—19 as (almost) exclusive paradigms for the will and activity of God in relation to human history. One of the results of this is that the distinction between the church and the world tends to be blurred, for wherever political liberation occurs God is seen as being at work.[63] Although, as was indicated at the outset of this chapter, South African Liberation Theology can, and must, be distinguished from Latin American Liberation Theology, a few comments regarding the use of these biblical texts may be useful.[64]

John Yoder has taken issue with those who have interpreted the Exodus narrative in the above way.[65] Firstly, he questions the particular interpretations that are derived from the Exodus narrative. He argues that the Exodus event was a miracle of divine intervention, which achieved the withdrawal of the Hebrew people from Egypt. It was not a human political programme of their take-over in Egypt. Moreover, the Exodus was preceded by the existence of a certain group of people who called upon the God of their fathers, and it was followed by the giving of the law at Sinai and the period of desert purification and teaching. As someone once put it, 'it was not enough to get the people out of Egypt but Egypt had to be got out of the people.'

Secondly, Yoder stresses that the Exodus cannot be regarded as a normative or authoritative paradigm (interpretative framework) because it was an exception.[66] In the Exile, for example, the Israelites were not commanded to rise up and leave; on the contrary, they were to plant vineyards and take wives (Jer. 29.1ff). Yoder then concludes by pointing to the goal of the church, to be a new and alternative community:

> Liberation is not a new king; we've tried that. Liberation is the presence of a new option, and only a non-conformed, covenated people of God can offer that. Liberation is the pressure of the presence of a new alternative, so valid, so coherent, that it can live without the props of power and against the stream of statesmanship. To *be* that option is to be free indeed.[67]

Yoder does not deny that liberation from sin, in all its individual and social manifestations, is an essential part of the Gospel. What he does, however, emphasise, is that in the search for political liberation the distinction between the Church and the world cannot, biblically speaking, be forgotten.

I, myself, am not convinced that the terms of 'liberation' and 'salvation' are interchangeable. Salvation always includes the elements of faith and obedience in response to the word or action of God, whereas liberation, especially socio-political liberation, does not necessarily involve faith and saving knowledge. Therefore, although salvation should certainly lead to the liberation of individuals from the power of evil and the transformation of oppressive societal conditions, socio-political liberation does not necessarily imply that the individual or his community has experienced the salvation of God. At this point I have strong reservations about some of the elements of the so-called 'Contemporary Pneumatology' and its accompanying understanding of the *Missio Dei*. God cannot be said to be behind any and every process of 'liberation', for such a view ignores both the issue of the *means* employed in some of these revolutionary movements and, I believe, the biblical emphasis of the activity of the Holy Spirit taking place through the *Church*. But, more of this in chapter seven.

Does a 'situational' hermeneutic mean that theological reflection is inevitably doomed to a treadmill within which nothing remains normative and authoritative, or is there some way out of the 'hermeneutical circle'?

Let us imagine a diagram consisting of two separate self-contained poles (X + Y), in between which several oblongs (Z) are poised. At one pole (X) represents the normative biblical revelation (consisting of as accurate a form of the Old and New Testament texts as we possess), while at the other (Y) represents the continually changing historical situations to which the text (X) claims to speak. Between the two poles an ongoing process of theological analysis, which must seek to relate to (X) (if it is to have any authority), and to (Y) (if it is to have any relevance) occurs.

THE HERMENEUTICAL COMPLEX

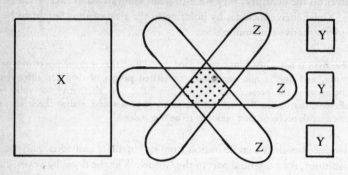

X   BIBLE
Y   DIFFERENT SITUATIONS
Z   DIFFERENT THEOLOGIES
[⋅⋅]   COMMON GROUND

This model could be seen as an alternative to both the vertical scripture-situation model and the hermeneutical circle. In such a model allowance is made for the existence of ideological influences, without regarding them as entirely inescapable (ie fully conditioning). It can also reduce the possibility of theological reflection becoming simply manipulative ideologising. In this model, the biblical revelation (X) is neither fully identified with human theology (Z) nor absorbed into the situations (Y).

It is for this reason that I do not agree that 'the Gospel *is* Liberation' any more than I would agree that it is 'the preservation of Law and Order'. The Christian faith includes the hope and task of liberation, but it also speaks of *the Church* as the suffering and persecuted community of God. Moreover, while it commands believers to pray for and honour the authorities, it does not command unquestioning obedience. Jesus himself seemed to have more sympathy with the Zealots than the Sadducees and Pharisees.[68] Both the protest of 'the poor' (in speaking of God only as the Liberator of the 'oppressed') and the triumphalism of the 'rich' (who speak of themselves as the recipients of God's blessing) may abuse the Gospel in order to justify their own aspirations or status. Neither the powerless nor the powerful can claim exclusive rights to God's support. Liberation is *a* hermeneutical key, but not the only one, and, like other attempts to make the Gospel relevent to a particular situation, is open to abuse. This is no excuse, however, for its insights to be ignored, or worse still rejected, because they are supposedly 'Communist-inspired'. For the Gospel does, and should, bring hope and liberation to those that embrace it.

The role of fellowship in the search for a valid interpretation and application of the scriptures must not be overlooked.[69] If the relevant groups are prepared to meet and relate with openness and a mutual desire for the truth, much invective and misunderstanding could be avoided. It is the particular tragedy of the Church in South Africa that, because it fails so dismally to be of one mind, one spirit and one purpose, its witness is dissipated by sectional loyalties, fears and aspirations. Unless true repentance and reconciliation occur, adequate social transformation and peace will recede into the realm of wishful thinking. The Church is not to be completely identified with society, nor can it rule society, but it is called to be a witness to, and model of, the far-reaching liberation that is to be found in Christ.

Notes

1 D Tutu, 'God intervening in human affairs' *Miss* 5:2 (1977) p115. For a fascinating insight into the life and thought of Bishop Tutu see John Webster (ed), *Bishop Desmond Tutu — the Voice of One Crying in the Wilderness* (London: Mowbray, 1982).

2. A Boesak and D Tutu, for example, attended the Pan African Conference of the Third World Theologians in Accra, Ghana, as late as 1977. For a recent discussion of Liberation Theology by a black South African cf Jerry Mosala, 'Liberation Theology' *LINK (TEEC) News* 14 (August, 1983) pp3—7. Two other black theologians who in recent years have developed liberation theologies much more influenced by Latin American thinkers than those presently under discussion, are Drs Simon S Maimela and Takatso A Mofokeng. Cf Mofokeng's *The Crucified among the Crossbearers* (Kampen: JH Kok, 1983).

3 JW de Gruchy, *The Church Struggle in South Africa*, p159.

4 J Cone, 'Black Theology and Black Liberation' in B Moore (ed), *The Challenge of Black Theology in South Africa*, p52.

5 B Moore, *ibid*, p ix. It is worthy of note that although Basil Moore (and Colin Collins) were important in the formation of the UCM and the setting up of the seminars on Black Theology, they are not mentioned by black theologians, many of whose writings do not adopt the tone of Moore's articles. It is a mistake to regard Moore's writings and some of the articles contained in *The Challenge of Black Theology* as representative of all Black Theology in South Africa. Nor would it appear to be valid to regard the content and tone of North American Black Theology as identical to that of South African Black Theology. This is precisely the mistake the C Boshoff and others make (see chapter seven).

6 A Boesak, *Farewell to Innocence* (Johannesburg: Ravan Press, 1977) p14.

7 A Boesak, 'Liberation Theology in South Africa' in K Appiah-Kubi and S Torres (eds), *African Theology en Route*, p173.

8 For an introduction to the so-called 'new hermeneutic' which is largely European in origin, and which stresses the role of *the interpreter* of the biblical texts see DA Carson, 'Hermeneutics: a brief assessment of some recent trends' *Ev RT* 5:1 (1981) pp 8—25, and AC Thiselton, 'The New Hermeneutic' in I Howard Marshall (ed), *New Testament Interpretation* (Exeter: Paternoster, 1977)

pp308—333. Marshall's book obviously emphasises the New Testament, but for a more philosophical and complex approach dealing with the major German figures see AC Thiselton, *Two Horizons* (Exeter, Paternoster, 1980). It must be stressed, however, that there are just a few of the vast array of articles and books on this subject.

9 René C Padilla, 'The Interpreted Word: Reflections on Contextual Hermeneutics' *Themelios* 7:1 (September 1981) p19. Padilla and Orlando Costas are representatives of the Evangelical wing of the Latin American Liberation Theologies.

10 Padilla, *ibid*, p18, and J Andrew Kirk, 'The use of the Bible in Interpreting Salvation Today: An Evangelical Perspective', *Ev RT* 1 (October, 1977) p3ff.

11 More than one book could be written on this subject alone: in this chapter a few issues which are important in South African Liberation Theology have been selected. For an introduction to some Latin American views cf G Gutierrez, *A Theology of Liberation*, (London: SCM, 1979) pp3—19, 43—77; L Boff, *Jesus Christ Liberator* (London: SPCK, 1981) pp33—48 and R Gibellini (ed), *Frontiers of Theology in Latin America,* (London: SCM, 1980) pp1—99. The more serious student should also consult the writings of people such as R Alves, J Miquez-Bonino, S Croatto, JL Segundo, etc.

12 Although Boesak distinguishes between 'situational' and 'contextual' in *Farewell to Innocence* p 17, these terms are usually used interchangeably. (Moreover, 'contextual' is generally preferred to 'indigenous').

13 *SASO Newsletter* (August, 1971) p17. See also A Boesak, 'Civil Religion and the Black Community' *JTSA* 19 (1977) pp35—44.

14 B Goba, 'Doing Theology in South Africa: A Black Christian Perspective' *JTSA* 31(1980) pp23—35.

15 A Boesak, 'Civil Religion and the Black Community' *JTSA* 19 (1977) p39. The commonly used term 'praxis' is derived from orthopraxy (true/valid action) and is contrasted with orthodoxy (true words/beliefs). Praxis emphasises commitment and participation in liberation, as well as resistance to oppression.

16 A Boesak, *Farewell to Innocence*, p16.

17 B Goba, *op cit*, pp32, 25

18 EK Mosothoane, 'The Use of Scripture in Black Theology' in WS Vorster (ed), *Scripture and the Use of Scripture* (Pretoria, Univ of SA, 1979) p32.

19 *Ibid*, p33. Mosothoane accuses Cone of precisely this tendency in his interpretation of Mt.5.17

20 *Ibid*, p35.

21 S Dwane, 'Christiology and Liberation' *JTSA* 35 (1981) p30.

22 JH Cone, *Black Theology and Black Power* (New York: Seabury Press, 1969) and *A Black Theology of Liberation* (Philadelphia: Lippincott, 1970).

23 E Mgojo, 'Prolegomenon to the Study of Black Theology' *JTSA* 21 (1977) pp27—28.

24 *Ibid*, p29. For a discussion of the sources of North American Black Theology, see GS Wilmore, *Black Religion and Black Radicalism* (New York: Doubleday and Anchor Press, 1973) p298ff.

25 *Ibid*, p31.

26 S Dwane *ibid*, p30.

27 For a similar view, see M Buthelezi's discussion of correlation in 'Change in the Church' *SAO* (August, 1973) p130.

28 D Roberts, 'Black Theology in the Making' *Rv Ex* (Summer, 1973) p231. Quoted by Mgojo in 'Prolegomenon to the Study of Black Theology' *JTSA* 21 (1977) p30.

29 A Mpunzi, 'Black Theology as Liberation Theology', in B Moore (ed) *The Challenge of Black Theology in South Africa,* p130ff.

30 M Buthelezi, 'The Christian Presence in Today's South Africa' *JTSA* 16 (1976) p7.

31 A Boesak, *Farewell to Innocence*, p113. Included in this is the liberation of whites, see Horst Kleinschmidt (ed), *White Liberation* (Johannesburg: Ravan Press, 1972).

32 A Boesak, *Farewell to Innocence* pp48—60.

33 *Ibid*, p59.

34 See E Baartman, 'The Significance of the Development of Black Consciousness for the Church' *JTSA* 2 (1973) p19ff; M Buthelezi, 'An African Theology or a Black Theology?' in B Moore (ed), *The Challenge of Black Theology for South Africa*, pp29—30; and S Dwane, 'Christology and Liberation' *JTSA* 35 (1981) pp29—31.

35 The events surrounding the riots and boycotts of 1976, together with the government's draconian clamp-down in October 1977 (when 18 organisations were banned and many individuals were restricted by banning orders and the like) greatly intensified black frustration and anger. This has certainly led to a radicalisation of both the tone and content of Black Theology.

36 See J Cone, *God of the Oppressed* (London: SPCK, 1977) p78ff.

37 B Moore, 'Towards a Black Theology' (unpublished paper) pp1—25.

38 A Boesak, *Farewell to Innocence*, p24.

39 H Riddebos, *The Coming of the Kingdom* (Philadelphia: 1962) p190, quoted by Boesak, *ibid*, p25.

40 EK Mosothoane, 'The Message of the New Testament seen in African Perspective' in H-J Becken (ed), *Relevant Theology for Africa* p60ff.

41 *Ibid,* p67.

42 A Zulu, 'Whither Black Theology? *Pro V* (March, 1973) p13. Boesak interacts with Zulu on this point in *Farewell to Innocence* pp111—2 and 115.

43 D Tutu, 'The Theology of Liberation in Africa', in K Appiah-Kubi and S Torres (eds), *African Theology en Route* , p166.

44 For further discussion of these see JW de Gruchy, *The Church Struggle in South Africa*, pp127—193, and D Bosch, 'Racism and Revolution: The Response of the Churches in SA', *Occasional Bulletin of Missionary Research* 3:1 (July, 1979) pp13—20.

45 'Pietists' is used here in the narrower and more perjorative sense of the word. 'Quietists' is sometimes used as an alternative term by other writers.

46 M Buthelezi, 'Christianity in SA' *Pro V* (15 June, 1973) p4. Cf also AD Mokoena, 'African Culture' *Pro V* (May, 1977) p10 and A Boesak, 'The Challenge for Christians in South Africa Today' *Pro V* (September 1977) pp11—12.

47 E Baartman, 'The Black Man and the Church' *Pro V* (March, 1973) p4. For a pertinent discussion of the present theological education of black seminary students see B Goba, 'The Task of Black Theological Education in South Africa', *JTSA* 22 (1978) pp19—30. Cf also S Ntwasa, 'The Training of Black Ministers Today' in B Moore (ed), *The Challenge of Black Theology in South Africa* pp141—146.

48 M Buthelezi, 'The Christian Presence in Today's South Africa' *JTSA* 16 (1976) p6 and S Gqubule, 'Can each Church remain United?' in M Nash (ed), *The Church and the Alternative Society* (SACC Papers, 1979) pp26—30.

49 See A Boesak, 'Civil Religion and the Black Community' *JTSA* 19 (1977) p44, *Farewell to Innocence* pp32, 49—50, 86—90 and 'The Black Church and the Future' in M Nash (ed), *The Church and the Alternative Society* p41.

50 S Gqubule 'What is Black Theology?' *JTSA* 8 (1974) pp21—22.

51 M Buthelezi, 'The Relevance of Black Theology' *SAO* (December, 1974) p198 and
    E Baartman, 'The Black Man and the Church' *Pro V* (April, 1973) p4. For a
    discussion on mixed worship by an Indian churchman cf E Mannikam, 'Mixed
    Worship is Necessary' *Pro V* (15 May, 1973) pp4—8.

52 A Boesak, 'He made us all but . . . Racism and the World Alliance of Reformed
    Churches' (WARC, Study Guide for Delegates 2) pp57—65. Reprinted in JNP Ser-
    fontein, *Apartheid, Change and the NG Kerk* (Johannesburg: Taurus, 1982),
    pp243—248.

53 S Buti, Report in *SAO*, 'The Acid Test' (August, 1978) p114. See also A Boesak,
    'Liberation Theology in South Africa' in K Appiah-Kubi and S Torres (eds) *African
    Theology en Route*, p 170 and de Gruchy, *The Church Struggle in South Africa*
    p179ff.

54 D Botha, 'Church and Kingdom in South Africa: Dutch Reformed Perspective' in
    M Nash (ed), *Your Kingdom Come* (SACC Papers, 1980) pp65—66. Also S Buti,
    'Crosscurrents and Crossroads in the South African Scene and the Kingdom of
    God' in M Nash (ed), *Your Kingdom Come,* pp7—10.

55 D Tutu, 'The Theology of Liberation in Africa' in K Appiah-Kubi and S Torres
    (eds), *African Theology en Route*, p167.

56 Simon S Maimela, 'The Atonement in the Context of Liberation Theology', *SAO*
    (December 1981) pp183—186. Reprinted in *JTSA* 39 (1982) pp45—54.

57 It is only in the more recent writings of both black and white theologians that the
    issue of the liberation of women is mentioned or discussed. Although this is likely
    to become more evident in Black Theology in South Africa (as it has elsewhere) a
    few articles can be mentioned here.
        The *SAO* issue of December, 1981 contained two important articles. The first
    was written by Mercy Amba Oduyoye (Lecturer at the University of Ibadan,
    Nigeria) entitled 'When the Woman is Human' pp188—190. The second was an
    interview with Busie Ncane Nhlegethwa (Secretary of the Women's Desk of the
    Council of Swaziland Churches) entitled 'Beyond the Rhetoric: Praxis at the
    Grassroots' pp190—192. Cf also Wilmore and Cone (eds), *Black Theology: A
    Documentary History, 1966—1979,* pp 363—444.
        A more recent South African work is WS Vorster (ed) *Sexism and Feminism in
    Theological Perspective* (Pretoria: UNISA, 1984).
        Another important development in Liberation Theology is Asian Liberation
    Theology, cf Wilmore and Cone (eds), *ibid*, p584ff.

58 Maimela, *op cit*, p184. For Maimela the terms 'liberation' and 'salvation' seem in-
    terchangeable, for he says: 'Put differently, the fundamental message of liberation
    theology is that the life, death and resurrection of Jesus Christ were aimed at the
    total liberation (salvation) of humanity from all kinds of limitations both spiritual
    and physical, and that this liberation is a dynamic historical process in which man
    is given the promise, the possibility and the power to overcome all the perverted
    human conditions on this side of the grave'(p185).

59 See a Latin American (Evangelical) view in Orlando E Costas, 'Evangelism and the
    Gospel of Salvation' *IRM* 63 (1964) pp24—37.

60 B Goba, 'Towards a "Black" Ecclesiology' *Miss* 9:2 (1981) p56. Elswhere he
    speaks of the Church as a 'servant of liberation', see 'Doing Theology in South
    Africa: A Black Christian Perspective' *JTSA* 31 (1980) p29.

61 B Goba, 'Towards a "Black" Ecclesiology' *ibid* p57.

62 For a helpful discussion on the inter-relationship between theology and ideology
    see C Villa-Vicencio, 'The use of Scripture in Theology: Towards a Contextual

Hermeneutic' *JTSA* 37 (1981) 3—22 and 'Where Faith and Ideology Meet: The Political Task of Theology', *JTSA* 41 (1982) 78—82.

63 Andrew J Kirk, *Liberation Theology: An Evangelical View from the Third World* (London: Marshall, Morgan and Scott, 1979) pp95—111 and 'The Use of the Bible in Interpreting Salvation Today: An Evangelical Perspective' *Ev RT* 1 (October, 1977) pp1—20.

64 There are, of course, many other issues that arise in some Latin American theologies such as the ideological alliance with Marxism and the use of its 'scientific' analysis of society, but these cannot be entered into here.

65 John H Yoder, 'Exodus and Exile: The Two Faces of Liberation' *Miss* 2:1 (1974) pp29—41. See also M Brenemen, 'The use of the Exodus in Theology' *Th FB* 3 (1974) pp5—9.

66 Yoder, *ibid*, p37.

67 *Ibid*, p41.

68 Cf O Cullman, *The State in the New Testament* (London: SCM, 1957), D Bosch 'The Church — The Alternative Community' *Be Transformed* 2:2, pp3—46 and John H Yoder, 'Jesus and Power' *Ecu R* 25:4 (October, 1973) pp447—454.

69 D Bosch, 'Racism and Revolution: The Response of the Churches in South Africa' *Occasional Bulletin of Missionary Research* 3:1 (July, 1979) p20.

CHAPTER SEVEN

White Theological Responses to Apartheid Ideology and Black Theology

In the preceding chapters the emphasis has been on the writings of black Christians. This chapter will point out important white reactions to these writings. My aim is to indicate that many of the criticisms articulated by black theologians against aspects of social life and Christian faith in South Africa are also found in the writings of certain white theologians. An indication of this agreement will not only serve as an important complement to the black critique of earlier chapters, but also forms an essential backdrop to specific white responses to the Black Theology of the past decade. Obviously, theologians who whole-heartedly support the Christian nationalism propagated in official government and (some) Church circles find the thinking of black theologians both offensive and dangerous.

White Theological Critiques of Civil Religion and Apartheid

It has often been said, with justification, that apartheid was not invented by the Nationalist Party. Nevertheless, it was that party that effectively formulated and legislated the separate existence of groups in South Africa, in a way never dreamed of, far less achieved, in earlier years. From the outset, these efforts were justified and even inspired by influential members of the NGK. As T Dunbar Moodie has incontrovertibly shown, the political policy of apartheid can by no means be separated from the Afrikaner civil religion which from the 1920s onwards pervaded the NGK.[1] However, all was not well within the laager, nor indeed outside it. For, from the earliest days of the formulation and implementation of the policy of apartheid, dissenting voices have been heard within both the Afrikaans and English churches.

Amongst the Afrikaner opponents were two eminent theologians of the NGK, Professors BB Keet and Ben Marais.[2] They were opposed to the notion that the distinct identity and self-preservation of Afrikaners should take precedence over the principle of Church unity and fellowship. They also envisioned the multitude of sufferings which blacks would undergo in the implementation of such a policy, and predicted that, rather than ensuring peace or stability as its architects promised, apartheid would result in ever-increasing conflict.[3] Professor Keet said:

> . . . it is my conviction that the time has come that our Afrikaans-speaking Churches should let the state know that they no longer see their way clear to continue with the apartheid policy and to insist that a better way of solving our racial problems be sought.[4]

Although Keet had expressed his views earlier, this quotation is taken from the controversial *Delayed Action*, a book issued by some leading Afrikaans theologians in 1961. In the same book, Professor Hugo du Plessis confronted the basic issue in these words:

> . . . self-preservation and a continuously underlying fear complex may not be the premise of our actions. Above everything else the Kingdom of God and its righteousness must be sought. If fear and self-preservation are the guiding principles in our personal and national lives, it is a demonstration of unbelief and leads to injustice and even oppression.[5]

In addition to these men, there were others in the English churches and especially in the Christian Council of South Africa (the forerunner of the SA Council of Churches) who also spoke out against the government's intentions.[6] Perhaps the best-known was Father Trevor Huddleston who published *Naught for Your Comfort* in 1956.[7] He not only argued against the theory behind the policy of apartheid but revealed the 'inside story' of the nature and effects of its implementation. With poignant detail he outlined the suffering which black people experienced in the cause of 'Christian' Afrikaner nationalism.

These initial criticisms were greatly intensified after the Sharpeville massacre in March 1960. A large crowd had gathered in front of the township police station to face arrest, having left their passes at home in defiance of the pass laws. The police later said that they regarded the crowd as dangerous and threatening (though this is debatable) and after some leaders were arrested, a few minutes of confusion ensued, in which stones were thrown and shots heard. Without being commanded to do so, several police opened fire and the rest followed suit. Within moments 69 people had been killed, mostly shot in the back, and 178 wounded.[8] After this tragic incident, boycotts and riots followed elsewhere and there was also an international outcry. (Who was to know then that a mere 16 years later, in Soweto, black children would also pay with their lives for protesting against all that apartheid stood for? Or, that incidents like these would later be repeated at Langa, Mamelodi and elsewhere.)

It was in this tense situation that the Cottesloe Consultation took place in Johannesburg (7—14 December, 1960). The Consultation had been called by the churches to discuss recent events and their own role in South Africa in the longer term. Although no agreement was reached regarding the ideology of apartheid itself, the Consultation did pass some significant resolutions, which contrasted with the prevailing policy of *separation* in Church and state, as is clear from the following:

> We recognise that all racial groups who permanently inhabit our country are a part of our total population, and we regard them as indigenous. Members of all these groups have an equal right to make their contribution towards the enrichment of the life of their country and to share in the ensuing responsibilities, rewards and privileges . . .

> No-one who believes in Jesus Christ may be excluded from any church on the grounds of his colour or race. The spiritual unity among all men who are in Christ must find visible expression in acts of common worship and witness, and in fellowship and consultation on matters of common concern.[9]

Although representatives of the Anglican, Congregational, Methodist, Presbyterian, Nederduitse Gereformeerde Kerk and Nederduitse Hervormde Kerk had signed the Consultation Statement, within days, members of the latter two churches (under pressure from the then Prime Minister, Dr Hendrik Verwoerd), Dr Koot Vorster and Dr Andries Treurnicht, began to dissociate themselves from it. Not everyone, however, bowed to the powers that be. Dominees Beyers Naudé, Albert Geyser and Ben Engelbrecht formed the Christian Institute in 1963. The Institute developed into a centre of Christian dissent and regularly published, as its mouthpiece, a journal called *Pro Veritate* ('on behalf of the truth').[10]

Another important document which contributed to the task of developing a theological critique of apartheid, as well as seeking to establish what the nature of the Church's response should be, was *The Message to the People of South Africa*, drawn up by a theological commission established by the SACC and issued in the name of the Council in 1968.[11] This booklet described the Gospel as a message which broke down the walls of division between people, and not one which erected and maintained them. The *Message* attacked apartheid for its policy of divisiveness and white supremacy and for preventing true Christian worship, fellowship and service from being exercised. The *Message* was followed a few years later by the Spro-cas (*Study Project on Christianity in Apartheid Society*) reports, which were published from 1970 onwards.[12]

The reports covered a variety of issues including political alternatives to apartheid, social problems, educational needs and the Church's identity and task. They were the work of people drawn from different churches, but united in the task of analysing the 'South African way of life' from a Christian perspective which was not bound by allegiance to one group or political ideology.

Like the Christian Institute, the Christian Council of South Africa (CCSA) was active throughout the 1960s. By 1968 it had changed its name to the South African Council of Churches (SACC) and played an increasingly prominent role in theological affairs.

As de Gruchy has pointed out, the SACC has been involved in a broad range of activities ranging from theological analysis to mission work, but its attempts to exercise a prophetic function have drawn criticism, even rejection, from many members of the public, and especially from the government.[13] The SACC initiated and published the *Message to the People of South Africa* and was involved in the raising of the issue of conscientious objection and the WCC's controversial 'Programme to Combat Racism'. Because the SACC and its staff are so often in the news and are constantly denounced by politicians as liberals or even Marxists, it is difficult to view this body with total objectivity. With regard to the SACC two points need to be noted. Firstly, the SACC has taken some pains to stress that it does *not* wholeheartedly support all the aims or theological views represented within the WCC. This fact must not be obscured by the irrelevant or inaccurate verbosity to which its opponents are sometimes prone. Secondly, the SACC viewpoint has its basis in a *theological* position. It regards apartheid not simply as a political policy, but a religio-ideological framework which encompasses and controls South African life and faith. If this framework is *unbiblical* it must also be heretical and dangerous for both the Church and the country. It is significant that the SACC and its opponents accuse each other of precisely the same thing: using religion for political ends and, until this issue is resolved, they will remain at loggerheads.

In 1977 a young group of Reformed Christians issued the 'Koinonia Declaration'. In it, they sought to respond *theologically* to issues related to South African society, voicing criticisms of government policy, and calling on it to pursue justice rather than simply imposing 'law and order'.[14]

In July 1979 more than 5000 Christians representing all the racial groups and many different denominations, met in Pretoria for the SACLA Conference (South African Christian Leadership Assembly). This week was a unique historical occasion, and must be seen as evidence of a growing concern and awareness that the Church must both 'put its house in order' and be a truly Christian witness to South Africa.[15] Although SACLA has been criticised by some in the Church for being 'bourgeois' and insufficiently radical, what was of special significance at this Conference was the general atmosphere of openness and fellowship amongst the delegates and speakers.

Attention must also be drawn to some recent joint publications from NGK churchmen and theologians. Of significance was *Storm-Kompas* (November, 1981), a collection of 24 essays and comments from members of the NGK.[16] Many of the writers take the NGK to task for its support of racial segregation and its close identification with Afrikaner national identity, the ruling Nationalist Party and the Afrikaner Broederbond. Although the contributers to *Storm-Kompas* did not speak with one voice the book, as could have been expected, caused a storm within the NGK and her sister churches. It appeared in the context of an ongoing, at times virulent, discussion within the NGK. Following on the debate concerning joint worship and mixed marriages, as well as the repercussions resulting from several individuals (such as Dr Jacques Kriel, Dr Willem Saayman and Professor Nico Smith) resigning from the NGK and joining the NGKA or NGSK, it was a continuation of the conflict between the *verligtes* and *verkramptes*.[17] Earlier, in October, 1980, eight NGK theologians had issued a statement which came to be known as the 'Witness of Eight'. It noted with concern and regret that the Church was failing to fulfil its reconciling task and even producing greater polarisation. Also, a call was made on members and officials of the NGK to strive for the 'elimination of loveless and racist attitudes and actions', solidarity with all Christians in need because of 'avoidable suffering' caused by social practices, economic imbalances and political measures. It also called for a 'form of church unity'.[18]

These events and documents were soon followed by others. The first was a Theological Conference held at UNISA (Pretoria) in January 1982,[19] at which various theologians made their contributions, either in talks, or from the floor. But, after Dr Pierre Rossouw's talk on the Wednesday, in which he defended apartheid as a political goal and a sound biblical principle, the Conference almost foundered. Several people took strong issue with the speaker and some considered a walk-out. Although the Conference continued, it all too clearly revealed that polarities in the Church were far from being reconciled.

The 'verligtes' did not let the grass grow under their feet, for, in June of the same year an 'Open Letter' (Die Ope Brief) signed by 123 people appeared in *Die Kerkbode*. The 'Open Letter' discussed the theological basis, and necessary practical implications, of reconciliation, church unity and the prophetic calling of the church. From points 2.2.1 to 2.2.7 virtually all the 'sacred cows' of the NGK are repudiated. These include the principle of 'eiesoortigheid' (one's own kind) which, they stress, cannot be defended scriptually nor employed as a political goal. Laws affecting mixed marriages, race classification and group areas are criticised, as well as forced removals, the system of migrant labour and the inadequate black education and poor housing which result from the implementation of apartheid.[20]

A few people reacted with glee, others (especially black NG leaders) with caution, but the vast majority of NG leaders and members were shocked and angry. The Broad Moderature literally refused to touch the Letter, and, on procedural grounds, refused to accept or discuss it at the Church's synod meeting.

Since then, a few of the signatories have published *Perspektief op die Ope Brief*,[21] but the stalemate between the 'verligte' and 'verkrampte' positions continues. Not even the declaration by the WARC (World Alliance of Reformed Churches) which met in Ottawa (1982) that apartheid should be regarded as a heresy, has budged those who believe that separate development has received divine sanction.

Therefore, it is difficult to assess to what extent, and how soon (if ever) thinkers such as these will be able to influence other leaders of the NGK (and the GK and NHK) as well as the larger group of church members. Nevertheless, it would appear to be valid to regard the people and events mentioned above as indicative of an important trend of self-criticism within the Afrikaner churches.

However, lest a false euphoria creep into this discussion, these developments must be viewed in relation to the government's commitment to maintaining the basic policy of separate development and, at the same time, seeking to incorporate Indian and Coloured people in the new Constitution. Moreover, the NGK remains officially committed to the 1974 Report on *Ras, Volk en Nasie en Volkereverhoudings in die Lig van die Skrif*.[22] The attitude of many Afrikaner theologians is perhaps typified by individuals such as Dr CWH Boshoff and Dr Treurnicht who, while they ostensibly reject racism and emphasise the need for the improvement of the black standard of living and opportunities, reject integration. They hold to the view that political and social change must take place within the context of the 'divine right of self-determination of nations', and remain firmly committed to a doctrinaire interpretation and strict enforcement of separate development[23] — a position which is slightly to the right of that of the government, but which enjoys support from the other Afrikaner political parties.

Besides these ideological debates, there is also the question of the attitudes and activities of local churches of both language groups, many of which continue to live in a make-believe world, giving little thought or attention to these issues. This is largely due, as was pointed out in chapters five and six, to a misunderstanding of the nature of the Christian faith. The majority of the church members in South Africa, according to Dr Hennie Pretorius, probably

. . . are people who feel that they are being true Christians by leading a life as virtuous as possible, by attending church services, by giving to the poor and to missions and by praying for missions. This group mainly believes that Christianity and politics are two separate areas and that the state should be allowed to be the state without interference by the church.[24]

Unless the broader challenge of the Gospel is more clearly perceived by the rank and file and lived out in a practical way, the views of a few senior leaders will have no effect anyway. The Church, as a whole, will then continue in its failure to practise what it preaches.

The Reaction to the Growth of Black Theology

One of the earliest responses in South Africa to Black Theology was a series of articles published in the Dutch Reformed theological journal. These also subsequently appeared as a booklet.[25] In these articles, Black Theology was largely assessed on the basis of the writings of Cone, Moore and articles by some black South Africans, later published in *Essays in Black Theology*.[26] Although Black Theology was weighed in the balance and largely found wanting, some positive comments were also made. Those elements of Black Theology which stressed the importance of blacks affirming their identity as blacks, or seeking to relate Christianity to their cultural background, were noted with approval.[27] D Crafford, while generally critical, admitted that white Christians failed to live in accordance with the Gospel that they preached, and Boshoff acknowledged the urgent need to improve the situation of black people.[28]

Despite these positive remarks, however, the general tone of the articles was censorious and many criticisms were advanced. Black Theology was regarded as being 'situationally bound' and therefore unable to separate itself from Black Power and Black Consciousness, and ultimately from a theology of revolution.[29] The writers saw Black Theology as being guilty of horizontalism in that it reduced the Gospel to socio-political liberation and neglected to take account of the Biblical emphasis on sin, salvation, conversion, spiritual rebirth, etc.[30] On these grounds, Boshoff warned that Black Theology could lead to the destruction of communication between black and white, and to violent social confrontation.[31] Finally, the acceptance of the principle of the separation of churches on ethnic lines as well as the separate training of ministers is implied throughout these articles.[32]

In 1974, E Hill, responding to the views expressed by these theologians, commended their swift response to Black Theology and especially D Crafford's acknowledgement that it revealed the failure of white Christians to live out the Gospel. Nevertheless, he argued that these writers failed to hear what was actually being said. He argued that Boshoff and Smith did not merely evade the challenge of Black Theology but failed, or refused, to see it:

They seem to be lacking in (group) self-knowledge and therefore to be incapable of either practising or giving a lead in group self-criticism — that is to say in repentence.[33]

Whites, Hill continued, needed to ask: 'what has given rise to Black Theology?' and until this was done, no progress could be made either in understanding or responding to it.

If it is possible to exonerate Prof Boshoff's early criticism of Black Theology on the grounds that in 1972 little was available in the way of black South African theological writing, his recent book *Swart Teologie: van Amerika tot in Suid Afrika* (1980) and his paper to the South African Missiological Society (1981) entitled 'Christ in Black Theology in a South African context' cannot be excused on these grounds.[34] His emphasis remains firmly fixed on North American Black Theology, and when he does turn his attention to South African Black Theology he evaluates it on the basis of some articles by Moore, the collection of essays edited by Moore (ie *The Challenge of Black Theology in South Africa*) and Boesak's *Farewell to Innocence*. Not only does he view Black Theology through the work of North American writers, regarding it very much in terms of a transplanted theology (as the title of his book indicates), but he also neglects to inter-act with other black South African writers. As a result, he does not discuss ways in which Boesak differs from Cone, nor whether other black South African theologians diverge from Boesak's perspective. Finally, he appears to remain convinced that Black Theology obscures the kernel of the Gospel (which he sees as being the forgiveness of sins and personal salvation) and threatens the Gospel by completely politicising it.[35]

Similar views are apparent in the 'Report of the Commission of Inquiry into the Mass Media' (1982) under the chairmanship of Judge MT Steyn. Volume 2 of this Report deals with African, Black and Liberation Theology at some length and provides a host of long quotations from the writings of several individuals. Despite their seeming exposure to many important books and articles by these theologians, the members of the commission come to several surprising conclusions. For example, much is made of John Mbiti's view that Black Theology will not become African Theology — a view that has been proved to be incorrect, at least in terms of black Africans in South Africa. The Report later proceeds to quote from Bishop Tutu's address at the 1977 Conference in Accra where he argues that in South Africa, Black Theology and African Theology come together, but without noting that Mbiti's and Tutu's views are mutually exclusive.[36]

Secondly, having shown that Bishop Tutu supports the development of an *African* Theology, which is sensitive to the needs and problems of Africans, the Report concludes that he is committed to 'differential development' in a

religious *and* political sense (which being interpreted means separate development!). Tutu is also interpreted as having rejected 'liberal' theology and
politics, including notions such as '. . . one man, one vote election of a central
government in a unitary but multiracial state. . .' — views which the bishop
will surely be astounded to have attributed to him.[37] What the bishop actually
says is that Africans must not uncritically accept Western interpretations of
Christian theology and think that as African Christians they have nothing to
contribute. Moreover, he is critical of the oppression that the South African
system holds for blacks. There is no indication in his writings that his
criticisms of aspects of Western Theology can by 'parity of reasoning' as the
Report claims, be transferred to 'Western liberal politicians and jurists'.
Similarly, Professor Setiloane's emphasis on *African* theology is, by the same
technique of 'parity of reasoning', made out to support a political dispensation
of differentiation and separation. The Report puts it like this:

> . . . the following words of *Prof Gabriel Setiloane* are fundamentally to the same
> effect *politically* as well as *theologically:* 'context-wise I believe we have now
> established the legitimacy of the African claim to a unique and different *theological*
> point of view within the ecumenical Christian community because of our cultural,
> geographical, spiritual, social and temperamental background.' Substituting
> 'political' for 'theological' and 'democratic' for 'Christian' in the above passage, the
> parity of effect is made quite clear.[38]

This is a clear case of putting words in someone's mouth.

Thirdly, little or no distinction is made between South African Black
Theology and the Black Theology of the USA, and, when these two approaches *do* coincide, for example, in their repudiation of injustice and
racism, the Report seems surprised.[39]

Finally, South African Black Theology is too readily and simplistically interpreted as being Marxist-inspired and pro-violence,[40] whereas it can be argued
that many of the political elements of South African Black Theology already
occur in the late 19th and early 20th century and thus pre-date Marxist influence. Moreover, as late as 1970, Black Theology, in its South African form,
was not directly linked to the Liberation Theology of Latin America where the
ideological alliance with Marxism is most apparent. Even today, black
theologians in South Africa have hardly embarked upon a *radical* class analysis
along Marxist lines.

All in all, the Report seems to be as ideologically bound as it claims are the
proponents of the theologies that it is discussing. Especially in terms of the
South African writers that it discusses, its interpretation often appears to be
either too dogmatic or the result of gross misinterpretation.

In contrast to the views of individuals such as Boshoff, or of the members of the Steyn Commission, Prof David Bosch, another Afrikaans theologian, came to rather different conclusions in his assessment of Black Theology. In 1972, he published an article on African and Black Theology in which he discussed the value of the work being done by blacks to 'Africanise' the Gospel.[41] He saw Black Theology as a reaction to the traditionally pietistic theology of Western missionaries and drew attention to its emphasis on a 'horizontal' salvation. He also observed that Black Theology, with its emphasis on the socio-political function of the church and the liberation of the oppressed, did have something in common with a theology of revolution, but he regarded the conclusion that the two are necessarily identical as unjustifiable and simplistic. Black Theology's stress on the black or African person, he admitted, was one-sided, but he went on to say that this should not be regarded as 'blatant anthropocentrism', but as a valuable corrective to previous pietistic theology. Finally, with respect to 'the message of reconciliation with God, the conversion of man's sinful heart and the salvation of sinners', he argued that, although more could be said of these in Black Theology, it would be false to claim that they are absent from it. Also in 1972, he reviewed *Essays in Black Theology* and, whilst he voiced several strong criticisms, he did not completely reject the approach taken. He concluded by saying that whites should read the book carefully and with humility, and that the issues brought up in it should be discussed and dealt with, rather than blithely ignored.[42] A few years later, Bosch read a paper in England on the subject of Black Theology. In it he dealt with the thought of a number of Black South African theologians and, again, while he expressed disagreement with some of their emphases, he said:

> . . . whatever whites have to say about Black Theology must be said in subdued tones. They will have to learn especially to submit their unquestioned assumptions to a severely critical test. And a study of Black Theology with an honest, open mind cannot but create in the white student an ever-increasing understanding of its deepest intentions.[43]

In 1974, PGJ Meiring, in his discussion of Black and African Theology, argued that both these theologies are, in part, a reaction to white domination, and expressive of a desire on the part of blacks to affirm their own identity. He went on to discuss, and agree with, another article by Bosch, in which he sought to outline both the positive and negative elements of Black Theology.[44] According to Meiring, the positive elements were the stress on the Christian faith as active service rather than quietism, and the criticism of the 'white man's Gospel' which he regarded as a sign of a greater creativity and maturity amongst black Christians. The negative elements were that there was a tendency for salvation to be understood in the category of this world alone, to underestimate the power of sin in man and to blame the whites for all that was being criticised and repudiated by blacks. In their conclusions, however, Meiring and Bosch speak of the need for humility by whites and blacks. Whites need to exercise humility because they are in no position to point an accusing finger and blacks need to remember the fallibility of all people.[45]

A year later, JJF Durand argued that Black Theology:

> . . . came in a certain sense as the religious answer for the frustrated black intelligentsia. His aspiration can now find a religious basis. Christianity, for which he retained an inherent respect, can now be loosed from its 'white enslavement'.[46]

He also argued that the future development of Black Theology was dependent not only on black theologians, but also on their perceptions of the reaction of white theologians. He rightly stated that:

> A negative rejection alone (however sound the theological reasons might be) without a true understanding of the background from which Black Theology sprang, without a critical self-examination and searching of heart, without a willingness to repentance for some basic issues of sociological, economical and political nature, will be of no avail and may lead to a breakdown in all communication.[47]

Never before, he concluded, had there been such an urgent need for real communication between the members of the Church of Christ.

Probably the most extensive treatment of South African Black Theology by a white theologian is John de Gruchy's excellent chapter on 'Black Renaissance, Protest and Challenge',[48] which is particularly useful because he analyses Black Theology within the larger framework of church history from the 17th century onwards. He does not make the mistake that some have, in seeing Black Theology merely as a recent development:

> Whatever its immediate cause, in an important sense black theology in South Africa began with the revolt of black Christians at the turn of the century, a revolt which found institutional expression in the African independent churches. Black theology is rooted in the on-going search by black Christians for authentic expressions of Christianity in South Africa. For this reason, it is wrong to suggest that there is a fundamental difference between what is now called African Christian theology and black theology.[49]

De Gruchy also deals accurately and sensitively with the immediate causes of and influences on Black Theology, both internal (such as Black Consciousness) and external (which include influences from Africa or the USA).

This brief survey of white theological reactions leads us on to an examination of the key features of the white response to Black Theology's teaching on Church and the Kingdom.

Liberation and The Church

Many white theologians have strongly affirmed that there can be no complete divide between Christianity and socio-political reality, and they have sought to define what the relationship between them should be. Throughout, however, there is an emphasis on the particular role of the Church in socio-political reality — rather than a blurring of the lines between the Church and the world.[50]

In 1976, FE O'Brien Geldenhuys affirmed the necessity for the church to play a role in liberation, but went on to say that its action should be governed by the biblical norms of love, justice, truth and peace. It should reject the prevalent, but false, identification of all secular movements of liberation with the Kingdom of God.[51]

Further, with reference to the NGK policy of emphasising the *volk* and the separation of churches along ethnic lines, Bosch has distinguished between the liberation of people and peoples, arguing that we 'have to ask in all seriousness whether the category of "people" or "nation" may be the object of the Church's concern for liberation.'[52] In the same article, Bosch emphasises that is is not possible to speak of liberation without the intervention of Yahweh in history and His establishment of a covenant community with responsibilities towards its own members as well as 'the poor, the stranger, the outcast, the exploited and the oppressed.'[53]

Elsewhere, Bosch has discussed the meaning of the phrase that the Church has to be in, but not of, the world. He argues that it must guard against becoming irrelevant (the withdrawal model), as well as becoming redundant, in that it has nothing particular to say to the world and becomes just another social agency.[54] Bosch views the role of the Church as many-sided: intercessor, witness, prophet and servant,[55] and discusses the meaning of the images of salt and light.[56] He maintains that the Church should never acquiesce in the face of the injustice and discrimination in South Africa.

Both Bosch and de Gruchy are concerned to view the socio-political function of the Church in the context of the Kingdom of God, and especially with respect to its eschatological tension (ie the tension between the Kingdom as already inaugurated but not yet consummated). According to de Gruchy,

> . . . the message of the Kingdom of God, centred in the person and proclamation of Jesus himself, relates to our personal and social existence and history today in its totality, as well as to our future.[57]

This eschatological tension between the 'already' and the 'not yet' is a strong feature of the work of Professor Ben Engelbrecht, and it stands in contrast to the view expressed by the black theologian S Dwane, at the 1980 SACC Conference. Whereas Engelbrecht would agree that the fact of the inauguration of the Kingdom must make a difference in the lives of believers, and in their efforts to proclaim and work out this salvation, he would strongly question Dwane's view that the Kingdom of God is 'the renewal of all creation' and 'the culmination of events in this life . . . the consummation of what God began at creation',[58] arguing that this fails to take sufficient cognisance of man's sinfulness and the limited extent of the believer's obedience to God. If this is true in relation to the Christian's individual life, how much more must it be so in relation to his socio-political context.[59] In other words, there can be no immediate or final liberation, in a personal or political sense, in this world. He goes on to emphasise that the 'not yet' of the Kingdom must be taken seriously, and that the Church must admit that the full nature of God's plan of salvation is not known, nor yet consummated. This means that there can be neither a simple identification of socio-political liberation with the activity of the Holy Spirit nor a Utopian hope that mankind can, itself, establish God's Kingdom on earth. Rather than speaking of a *nova creatio*, which calls for an overthrow of the existing order, the Church must speak of a *re creatio* in which present circumstances are preserved or transformed, according to their conformity to God's purposes. The Church presently experiences only the first fruits of the Spirit (Romans 8.23) which are the guarantee of the Kingdom which has *yet* to be consummated. He is critical, therefore, of the perfectionism, intolerance and impatience of Liberation Theology in its expectation of, and demand for, an immediate and 'total' liberation.[60]

This does not mean, however, that Engelbrecht believes that the Church should sink into compliance with the world. On the contrary, it is called to the continuous and urgent task of seeking to bring every aspect of life, individual and societal, into conformity with the will of God as revealed in the Scriptures.

As can be seen from the above discussion, there have been various reactions to South African Black Theology. In the nature of the case, much of the discussion has ranged within academic circles and, therefore, the full impact of black theological thinking has not been felt at the local church level. This is especially true of the 'white' churches. It is hoped that this book will help to broaden the discussion and thereby facilitate further awareness of and involvement in the task of establishing Church unity, social justice, liberty and peace.

Notes

1 T Dunbar Moodie, *The Rise of Afrikanerdom: Power, Apartheid and the Afrikaner Civil Religion* (London and Berkeley: Univ of California Press, 1975). Cf also WA de Klerk, *Puritans in Africa: A Story of Afrikanerdom* (Harmonds-

worth: Penguin, 1975). Civil Religion in this case may be defined as the belief that the history of the Afrikaner reveals the will and work of God and is not just the result of human ideas and effort. Consequently, the preservation and continuation of the *volk* (people) is also a matter of Divine purpose. Cf Moodie, *ibid*, p1.

2 See J de Gruchy, *The Church Struggle in South Africa* p58ff and E Regehr, *Perceptions of Apartheid: The Churches and Political Change in South Africa* (Kitchener, Ontario: Between the Lines, 1979) p177ff.

3 See BB Keet, *Whither South Africa?* (Stellenbosch, 1956) and Ben Marais, *Colour: the Unsolved Problem of the West* (Cape Town, 1952). Cf also AS Geyser *et al* (eds), *Delayed Action* (Pretoria: NG Kerkboekhandel, 1961).

4 BB Keet, 'The Bell has already Tolled' in AS Geyser *et al* (eds), *Delayed Action* p11. Cf also Ben Marais, 'The Church in the Contemporary World' in *Delayed Action*, pp29—42.

5 H du Plessis, 'The New Era and Christian calling regarding the Bantu in South Africa' in *Delayed Action*, p67.

6 For further details regarding the Christian Council of South Africa see E Regehr, *Perceptions of Apartheid*, p159.

7 T Huddleston, *Naught for your Comfort* (London: Collins, 1956).

8 Regehr, *op cit*, p187ff.

9 *Cottesloe Consultation* (The Report of the Consultation among South African Member Churches of the World Council of Churches) 7—14 December 1960 at Cottesloe, Johannesburg, p74.

10 The CI was banned in October, 1977. Cf J de Gruchy, *The Church Struggle in South Africa*, pp103—115.

11 *The Message to the People of South Africa* was published by the SACC in June, 1968. It was followed by 'A Biblical Commentary on the *Message to the People of South Africa*' edited by the Rev J Davies and published by the Christian Institute. Thereafter, *The Message in Perspective: a Book about the Message to the People of SA* was brought out by the SACC.

12 eg *Towards Social Change* (no 6) *Power, Privilege and Poverty* (no 7) and *Apartheid and the Church* (no 8).

13 de Gruchy *op cit*, p115ff.

14 'The Koinonia Declaration' was subsequently published in *JTSA* 24 (1978) pp58—64. For a response to this Declaration see the 'Response' by members of the *Missiological Society* in *JTSA* 30 (1980) pp68—71.

15 Cf the entire volume of *JTSA* 29 (1979) for reports and papers. SACLA had been preceded, and largely inspired by, PACLA (The Pan African Christian Leadership Assembly) which met in Nairobi in 1977. Cf M Cassidy and Luc Verlinden, *Facing the New Challenges: The Message of PACLA* (Kisumu, Kenya: Evangel Publishing House, 1978).

16 Nico J Smith, FE O'Brien Geldenhuys and Piet Meiring (eds), *Storm-Kompas* (Cape Town: Tafelberg, 1981).

17 Cf JNP Serfontein, *Apartheid, Change and the NG Kerk* (Johanesburg: Taurus, 1982) pp135—194.

18 *Ibid*, p153.

19 *Ibid*, pp176—181.

20 *Ibid*, pp275—278.

21 David J Bosch, Adrio König, Willem D Nicol (eds), *Perspektief op die Ope Brief* (Johannesburg: Human and Rousseau, 1982).

22 The rather misleading official translation of this title is *Human Relations and the*

South African Scene in the Light of Scripture (Cape Town: DRC Publishers, 1976). For a detailed critique see D Bax, *A Different Gospel: A Critique of the Theology behind Apartheid* (Johannesburg: The Presbyterian Church of SA 1979?).

23 For another view of South Africa's political options see F van Zyl Slabbert and David Welsh, *South Africa's Options: Strategies for Sharing Power* (Cape Town; David Philip, 1979, and London: Rex Collings, 1979).

24 H Pretorius, ' "White" South African Ecclesiology' *Miss* 9:1 (1981) pp29—30. Also see an excellent article by D Bosch entitled 'Racism and Revolution: Response of the Churches in South Africa' *op cit* pp13—20.

25 CWH Boshoff, 'Die Betekenis van die Swart Teologie vir Kerk en Sending in Suid-Afrika: Die Swart Teologie as Bevrydingsbeweging' *NGTT* 14:1 (1973) pp5—20; PES Smith, 'Swart Teologie en die Sending van die Kerk' *NGTT* 14:1 (1973) pp21—35 and D Crafford, 'Swart Teologie en die Ned Geref Kerk in Afrika' *NGTT* 14:1 (1973) pp36—47. The booklet was *Swart Teologie* (Pretoria: NGK Boekhandel, 1972).

26 Referred to in this book as *The Challenge of Black Theology in South Africa*, B Moore (ed).

27 C Boshoff, *ibid*, pp6—8 and P Smith, *ibid*, p29ff.

28 D Crafford, *op cit*, p37 and Boshoff *ibid*, p19.

29 P Smith, *op cit*, p25 and Boshoff *ibid*, pp13,18.

30 P Smith, *ibid*, p26ff. Smith was also, and rightly, critical of S Ntwasa and B Moore's treatment of the concept of the authority of God. This is, however, not a recurring theme in subsequent black theological writings in South Africa.

31 C Boshoff, *op cit*, pp5, 18.

32 D Crafford, *op cit*, pp42, 46 and P Smith, *op cit*, p34.

33 E Hill, 'The Impenitent Ostrich' *SAO* (March, 1974) p42.

34 *Swart Teologie: van Amerika tot in Suid-Afrika* (Transvaal: NG Boekhandel, 1980) and 'Christ in Black Theology in a South African Context '(paper read at the SA Missiological Society Annual Congress, Potchefstroom, 1981). This paper roused a storm of protest from the delegates at the Congress.

35 *Swart Teologie: van Amerika tot in Suid-Afrika,* pp105—117 and 129.

36 'Report of the Commission of Inquiry into the Mass Media', Vols 1—3 (1982) under the chairmanship of Judge MT Steyn, pp88ff, 640ff (hereafter referred to as the *Steyn Commission*).

37 *Ibid,* pp631—643 and 653—5. Cf D Tutu, 'Black Theology/African Theology — Soul Mates or Antagonists?' in GS Wilmore and JH Cone (eds), *Black Theology: A Documentary History: 1966—1979* pp483—491 and 'The Theology of Liberation in Africa' in K Appiah-Kubi and S Torres (eds), *African Theology en Route* pp162—168.

38 *Steyn Commission* pp655 and 646—657.

39 *Ibid,* pp87ff, 593ff and 658—678.

40 *Ibid,* pp 587ff and 608ff. I have not entered into a discussion of the issue of Black Theology and violence, for two reasons: firstly, it is a topic so large and complex that it could not be dealt with adequately here; secondly, as a result of the fact that blacks are not free to express themselves fully on this subject, it would probably be a rather fruitless exercise. Generally speaking, however, it is probably valid to say that black theologians tend to point out the uncritical stance of whites regarding military and police activity. They also show great reluctance to espouse the call for violent revolution voiced by many black radicals unconnected with the Church. Cf

A Boesak, *Farewell to Innocence* pp48—59 amd 98—117 and D Tutu, 'God Intervening in Human Affairs' *Miss* 5:2 (1977) pp111—117.

41 D Bosch, 'Inheemswording, Afrikanisasie en Swart Teologie', *NGTT* 13:2 (1972) pp103—115.

42 D Bosch, 'The Case for Black Theology' *Pro V* (15 August, 1972) pp3—9.

43 D Bosch, 'Currents and Crosscurrents in South African Black Theology' reprinted in GS Wilmore and JH Cone (eds), *Black Theology: A Documentary History (1966—1979),* p235.

44 P Meiring, 'Die Agtergrond van Swart Teologie in Afrika en Suid-Afrika' *Bulletin* 6 (1974) p11 and D Bosch, 'Swartze Theologie in Sudafrika' *Evangelische Missions Magazin* 117: 1/2 (1973) pp77—84.

45 Meiring, *ibid* p11.

46 JJF Durand, 'Black Theology in a South African Context' *Theological Bulletin* 3:2 (May, 1975) p4.

47 *Ibid,* p7—8.

48 In *The Church Struggle in South Africa,* pp149—193. First published by Eerdmans, Grand Rapids, in 1979. The South African edition was published by David Philip in Cape Town in the same year.

49 de Gruchy, *ibid,* p156.

50 For a discussion of this in relation to the evangelical and ecumenical models see D Bosch, *Witness to the World: The Christian Mission in Theological Perspective,* pp202—229 and 'In Search of Mission; Reflections on "Melbourne" and "Pattaya" ' *Miss* 9:1 (1981) p3—18.

51 'The Church's Role in Liberation' in D Thomas (ed), *Liberation* (SACC Papers, 1976) pp42—43.

52 D Bosch, 'The Church and the Liberation of Peoples?' *Miss* 5:2 (1977) pp33,34. This statement was strongly objected to by CI van Heerden in his response to Bosch, cf pp41—42 of the same journal. For further discussion see de Gruchy, *The Church Struggle in South Africa,* pp200—217 and JNP Serfontein, *Apartheid, Change and the NG Kerk,* pp255—259.

53 D Bosch, *ibid,* p37.

54 D Bosch, 'The Church as the "Alternative Community" ' *JTSA* 13 (1975) pp3—11.

55 D Bosch, 'The Church in South Africa — Tomorrow (Part 2) — Seeking a way out of the dilemma' *Pro V* (September, 1975) p11ff.

56 D Bosch, 'The Kingdom of God and the Kingdoms of this World' *JTSA* 29 (1979) p10ff.

57 Bosch, *ibid,* pp8—13 and de Gruchy, *op cit,* p198. In fact, the whole of de Gruchy's final chapter deals with the Kingdom, cf pp195—237.

58 S Dwane, 'Black Christianity in Kingdom Perspective' in M Nash (ed), *Your Kingdom Come* (SACC Papers, 1980) p39.

59 Personal communication. Whereas much of Engelbrecht's work has concentrated on thinkers such as J Moltmann, H Ott and JM Lochman, etc, much of what he says in applicable to Black Liberation Theology. These ideas, and others, are worked out in his book *God en die Politiek* (Butterworth, 1978) and the articles 'The Indwelling of the Holy Spirit: An Evaluation of Contemporary Pneumatology' (Part 1) *JTSA* 30 (1980) pp19—33. 'Part 2: A Contemporary Statement' *JTSA* 31 (1980) pp36—45.

60 Engelbrecht, *ibid,* p41ff.

Conclusion

In this book, I have sought to describe and analyse the origins, growth and main features of what can broadly be termed South African Black Theology. Despite obvious differences in terms of interest and content, the various elements that go to make up South African Black Theology are integrated by two factors: the black identity of its writers and by their desire to understand *and* apply the Christian faith. It is, therefore, a disservice to and a misunderstanding of its deepest intentions for it to be blithely dismissed as syncretic or subversive.

In order for South African Black Theology to be correctly understood and fairly assessed, the following four factors must, I believe, be borne in mind. The reader must be disposed to listen before he or she judges, distinguishing between the various major strands of South African Black Theology (eg Africanisation and Liberation). The reader should also become aware of the differing aims, tone and content of the many black theologians in South Africa. Finally, he or she must recognise that, although Black Theology interacts with related theologies in Africa and the Americas, South Africa has its own history. Its black theologians draw on this common experience and select, on the basis of their own insights, those elements of Christian theology which they find to be relevant and valid.

Thus, in chapter one it was shown that although the term 'Black Theology' is a new one, many of its concerns date back to an earlier period. By the beginning of the 20th century its major elements (such as Africanisation, the Independent Churches and emphasis on the broader social implications of the Gospel) were already evident. Amongst other things, this means that to regard Black Theology as the result of recent liberal or communist infiltration amongst blacks, by 'outside elements', is patently false. Whatever external influences there have been, or will be, Black Theology is firmly rooted in the historic and on-going resistance to European domination of black existence, whether political, economic, cultural or religious. Moreover, in relation to black grievances or aspirations, this fact severely weakens, even eliminates, the on-going white justification that 'these things take time, Rome was not built in a day . . .'

Having established the early foundations of South African Black Theology, the next step was to relate it to a broader theological context. It was shown that South African Black Theology has been influenced by, and interacts at a number of points with, African Theology, the Black Theology of the USA and, to a lesser extent, Latin American Liberation Theology.

Thus, South African Black Theology shares with the African Theology of the rest of the continent a concern to develop an *African* Christianity, ie how to understand and live the Christian faith without being compelled to negate one's African-ness. This is especially true with respect to Africa's rich cultural heritage, which Christians wish to be free to express in ways that are compatible with Christian belief, rather than in conformity with Western patterns and practices.

In common with the Black Theology of the USA, South African Black Theology has affirmed the importance of black identity, rejected racism and questioned the nature and value of integration. It has not, however, agreed with those American writers who speak of black nationalism (and tend towards reverse racism), nor has it broken off contact with the white churches. But it has strongly emphasised the need for repentance, radical changes and meaningful reconciliation.

The modern form of the liberationist theme in South African Black Theology, while it has affinities (and increasingly so) with the various Latin American writers, especially with respect to the use of liberation as a hermeneutical key, was initially introduced by the black American, James Cone. Significantly, the extensive 'ideological alliance' between the vast majority of Latin American liberation theologians and Marxist ideology, is at present not found to any great extent amongst the black South African theologians.

South African Black Theology thus uniquely incorporates the African, Black and Liberation Theologies, for, where else do these come together in quite the same way? Moreover, South African Black Theology is part of the world-wide theological response of the so-called Third World churches to the situations in which they find themselves. These 20th century theologies are the fruit of the amalgamation, and interchange, between Christianity and the broad social practices and world views it has encountered (and which have accompanied it), in its task of world mission. As a consequence, Western theologians must not be too hasty in their judgements. Not only are these theologies relatively new (in the context of nearly 20 centuries of Church history) but 'Western' Christianity must also beware that it does not denigrate them whilst ignoring its many own failures.

The Africanist theme in South African Black Theology is, to my mind, a welcome one. It is an inevitable and much-needed development (in view of the large African population) in terms of both those who have already been reached by the Gospel, and those who have yet to hear and respond to it. As was pointed out in chapter three, the Africanist theme concentrates largely on matters related to African traditional religion and culture, but does not exclude discussion of the expressly political implications of the Christian faith for the whole of the African continent. I have also tried to indicate the various views and interests of different African theologians in order to guard against the analysis becoming over-simplified and inaccurate. It must always be recognised that African Theology, even in a particular country, such as South Africa, is broad-ranging and encompasses the beliefs and customs of a large variety of people. African Theology, therefore, needs to effectively relate to the many different tribal beliefs, to rural and urban populations, to the educated and the uneducated, and to those who are and are not politicised.

Whereas I accept the need to express the Christian faith in appropriate African forms, certain problems may and do arise. The first of these, of which much has already been made by others, is syncretism. Syncretism occurs when the Christian Gospel is distorted or abused by an indiscriminate mixing of its beliefs and forms with that of another religion. The danger is, I feel, less prevalent than has previously been made out, especially in the light of the fact that several Afrcan theologians are aware of this problem, and are concerned to eliminate or, at least, limit its manifestations. While this may yet take time, it is a danger against which many (even in the oft-maligned African Independent Churches) are guarding themselves. To my mind the greater threat is that of further separation between Churches which can so easily develop from the emphasis on a certain group's *culturally expressed* Christian faith. Worse still, it can be and has been used by other parties to justify political segregation. I would argue, therefore, that whilst we should not embark on a doctrinaire rooting out of diversity in the Church, issues such as language, culture and class should not be used or allowed to prevent the unity of the Church being practically expressed. This would be a valuable means of removing ignorance, suspicion and fear, promoting mutual understanding, repentance and true Christian love. If such fellowship were wide-spread it could also issue in a commitment to justice, mutual service and much needed societal transformation.

With regard to the AICs I was, unfortunately, able only to scratch the surface of this fast-growing field of faith and study. As is apparent from recent research, the independent churches in Africa have achieved a great deal in terms of evangelism, worship, fellowship and caring services. The present trend is to view the AICs in a more positive light than was the case amongst some earlier researchers and theologians. However, until further research is forthcoming with regard to the extent of the specifically *Christian* content in the teachings and practices of the AICs, a final assessment would be premature. Finally, the political elements within the AICs, especially at their outset, were shown to be part of the resistance to white rule in all areas of life. In this sense, the politicisation of the Gospel by blacks in South African is no new phenomenon.

Black Theology, in the sense of a search for black awareness or identity, is an essential aspect of the theological thinking of blacks on this continent. Even amongst those who prefer to call themselves African theologians, the issue of black consciousness and identity is quite simply a reality *because of* the constant stress on race in South Africa. This theme within South African Black Theology is inextricably linked with the desire, amongst these Christians, for the Christian faith to be contextualised. They believe that Christianity cannot have meaning and value for blacks unless it has a message that speaks to their vital concerns. Christianity, they argue, cannot be regarded as being faithfully lived out if a person (or a group) simultaneously practises racism. More especially, in terms of the Church, reconciliation and hatred of another race or group *cannot* co-exist. It has been pointed out that in contrast to the Black Theology of the USA, South African black theologians have exhibited a great deal of restraint and patience. Thus, although the possibility exists of Black Theology tending towards an uncritical affirmation of black solidarity and power, there is little indication that this is either a common practice or an aim. The more threatened a white reader himself, or herself, is, the more threatening Black Theology will appear, despite its best intentions.

As a consequence of the internal dynamic of Black Consciousness and the widespread acceptance of the meaning expressed in the slogan 'Black is Beautiful', Black Theology is not about to die out. As long as the need for the affirmation of personal identity exists, and particularly in a society where some people are regarded as 'non-whites' or 'non-Europeans' or, indeed, non-persons, the acceptance of black identity as created by God will remain part of the attraction and value of South African Black Theology.

It is perhaps Black Liberation Theology that poses, from the viewpoint of those who uncritically affirm the status-quo, the greatest threat to Church and

State in South Africa. It can, however, also be regarded as the greatest challenge to the Church, ie to *be* the new community of God's people, and to effectively communicate His will to the world. It is at this point that the importance of the hermeneutical debate becomes apparent, for who are part of this new community, and what is God's will for the world? Is the church to be exclusively made up of '*ware* Afrikaners', 'the oppressed black masses' or 'English-speaking liberals'? Surely not. Why is it, then, that while much is made of the unity of the Church, this fails to take concrete and meaningful form in the lives of individual believers and at a synod level? White people cannot both have their cake and eat it, it is not valid to question black solidarity as exclusive or subversive and, simultaneously, to practise segregation and dominance.

Moreover, if the distinction between Church and State becomes blurred, as is presently the case in that separate development is promoted by the NGK, it is only to be expected that calls for religious change will be regarded as political threats. The true state of affairs is not merely that Liberation Theology politicises Christianity, but that it questions the present (Afrikaner) politicisation of Christianity. Whether Liberation Theology will itself land up in a similar ideological trap, but on the left of the political spectrum, remains to be seen.

Let us take up this second question for a moment. In order to remain Christian, Liberation Theology must begin by examining what 'liberation' means. To do this it naturally turns to the Bible, which it interprets by employing the hermeneutical key of liberation. But this is a circular argument and, therefore, a circular process. Indeed, we find ourselves within the hermeneutical circle. This is why, in chapter six, I regard liberation as *a* hermeneutical key within the total process of theologising, which also includes the thoughts of other theologians who are in different situations, and who claim the authority of the Bible for their own conclusions. Once this picture becomes clear in our minds, the effect of continued ideological and partisan influences in the doing of theology also becomes apparent. Having acknowledged this, theologians are then freed from enslavement to these interests and are able to both *utilise* and *criticise* the questions and solutions which arise out of their varying contexts. The only preconditions are integrity, mutual respect and true fellowship. It was the difficulties that these preconditions present in the South African situation that were analysed in chapter seven.

Finally, my discussion of the reactions of white theologians to Black Theology has revealed the polarity between those who show a willingness to be self-critical and to admit that they need to learn from black theologians, and those who do not seem to wish to do this. It would appear that unless theologians are going to be content to continue shouting fruitlessly from within their isolated perspectives (and thereby further sacrifice the unity and integrity of the Church to partisan interests), there must be a concrete effort to jointly search out, and mutually submit to, the revealed will of the Lord of the Church. This can only be done if theologians and church members admit that their understanding of God's will is imperfect and open to correction, ie to confess that their theologies are not necessarily fully identifiable with the Bible. This will be no easy task, and the history of the Church in South Africa should stand as a warning and lesson to the blithely optimistic, but it remains the task to which Christ has called His Church, and for which He has empowered it. Unless significant steps are taken to prevent the further subversion of the Church's unity and witness, the Body of Christ will continue to be broken by segregation and conflict. This would be a blatant denial of what the Church is called to be and open defiance of Christ's command to be one in faith, worship and witness.

Bibliography

a) BOOKS AND ARTICLES

ADEYEMO, Tokunboh (1978), 'Contemporary issues in Africa and the Future of Evangelicals'. In *Ev RT* Vol 2 No 1 (1978) pp2—13.

ANDERSON, Gerald H & STRANSKY, Thomas F (eds) (1976), *Mission Trends No 3: Third World Theologies.* New York & Grand Rapids: Paulist & Eerdmans, 1976.

ANKRAH, Kodwo E (1980), 'Political Violence and Social Injustice in Southern Africa: Some Issues facing African Theologians and Churchmen', In *Ecu R* Vol 32 (1980) pp29—39.

APPIAH-KUBI, Kofi (1975), 'The Church's Healing Ministry in Africa'. In *Ecu R* Vol 27 (1975) pp230—239.

APPIAH-KUBI, Kofi & TORRES, Sergio (eds) (1979), *African Theology en Route (Pan African Conference of Third World Theologians, Accra, Ghana, 1977).* Maryknoll, NY: Orbis Books 1979.

BAARTMAN, Ernest (1973), 'The Significance of the Development of Black Consciousness for the Church'. In *JTSA* Vol 2 (1973) pp18—22.

— (1973), 'Black Consciousness'. In *Pro V* March 1973 pp4—6.

— (1973), 'The Black Man and the Church'. In *Pro V* April 1973 pp3—5.

— (1975), 'The Reconciling Hypocrite'. (Paper read at the Consultation of ASATI Staff Institute, Rosettenville, 16 January 1975). MS 17pp.

— (1976), 'Response' [to FE O'Brien Geldenhuys]. In Thomas (1976) pp47—52.

BAX, Douglas S (1979?) *A Different Gospel: A Critique of the Theology behind Apartheid* (Johannesburg, Presbyterian Church of SA, 1979?)

— (1983), 'The Tower of Babel in South Africa Today'. In *JTSA* Vol 42 (1983) pp51—55.

BECKEN, Hans-Jürgen (ed) (1973), *Relevant Theology for Africa (Report on a Consultation of the Missiological Institute at Lutheran Theological College, Mapumulo, Natal, September 12—21, 1972)*. Durban: Lutheran Publishing House 1973.

BECKLEY, Rex (1973), 'The Race Dilemma in the Church: Sydney in Perspective'. In *Pro V* February 1973 pp13—17.

BIKO, Steve (1974), 'Black Consciousness and the Quest for a True Humanity'. In Moore (1974) pp36—47.

— (1978), *I write what I like*. London: Heinemann 1978.

BLUNK, J (1975), 'Freedom'. In Brown (1975) pp715—721.

BOESAK, Allan A (1973), 'Is Apartheid Kerke se Skuld?'. In *Pro V* February 1973 pp21—23.

— (1974), 'Waarheen wil swart teologie?', In *Pro V* February 1974 pp5—7.

— (1976), *Farewell to Innocence: A Socio-Ethical Study of Black Theology and Black Power*. 2nd edition; (1st edition The Netherlands: JV Kok 1976; also published under the title *Black Theology Black Power* London: Mowbrays 1978); Johannesburg: Ravan 1977.

— (1977a), 'Swart Bewussyn, Swart Mag en "Kleurling Politiek"; Black Consciousness, Black Power and "Coloured Politics" '. In *Pro V* February 1977 p9—12.

— (1977b), 'Civil Religion and the Black Community'. In *JTSA* Vol 19 (1977) pp35—44.

— (1977c), 'The Challenge for Christians in South Africa Today'. *Pro V* September 1977 pp11—13.

— (1979a), *The Finger of God: Sermons on Faith and Responsibility*. Johannesburg: Ravan Press 1979.

— (1979b), 'Liberation and Theology in South Africa'. In Appiah-Kubi & Torres (1979) pp169—175.

— (1980a), 'The Black Church and the Future'. In Nash (1980) pp39—48. Also in *Ecu R* 32 (1980) pp16—24.

— (1980b), 'A View from South Africa'. In *The Banner* No 29 December 1980 pp14—16.

— (1980c), 'Mission to those in Authority (A letter to the South African Minister of Justice)'. In *IRM* Vol 69 (1980) pp71—77.

BOFF, Leonardo (1972), *Jesus Christ Liberator: A Critical Christology of Our Time*. ET (Spanish original Petropolis: Brazil 1972) London: SPCK 1980.

BOSCH, David J (1972a), 'Inheemswording, Afrikanisasie en Swart Teologie'. In *NGTT* Vol 13 No 2 (1972) pp103—115.

— (1972b), 'The case for Black Theology'. In *Pro V* 15 August 1972 pp3—9.

— (1973a), 'God in Africa: Implications for the Kerygma'. In *Miss* Vol 1 No 1 (1973) pp3—20.

— (1973b), 'God Through African Eyes'. In Becken (1973) pp68—78.

— (1975a), 'The Church in South Africa — Tomorrow Part 1'. In *Pro V* August 1975 pp4—6.

— (1975b), 'The Church in South Africa — Tomorrow Part 2'. In *Pro V* September 1975 pp11—13.

— (1975c), 'The Church as the "Alternative Community" '. In *JTSA* Vol 13 (1975) pp3—11.

— (1977a), 'The Church and the Liberation of Peoples?' In *Miss* Vol 5 No 2 (1977) pp8—39.

— (1977b), 'The Church: The Alternative Community'. In *Be Transformed* Vol 2 No 2 (1977?) pp3—45.

— (1978), 'Renewal of Christian Community in African Today'. In Cassidy & Verlinden (1978), pp92—102.

— (1979a), 'Racism and Revolution: The Response of the Churches in South Africa'. In *Occasional Bulletin of Missionary Research* Vol 3 No 1 (July 1979) pp13—20.

— (1979b), 'Currents and Crosscurrents in South African Black Theology'. In Wilmore & Cone (1979), pp220—237.

— (1979c), 'The Kingdom of God and the Kingdoms of this World'. In *JTSA* Vol 29 (1979) pp3—13.

— (1980), *Witness to the World: The Christian Mission in Theological Perspective*. London: Marshall Morgan & Scott 1980.

— (1981), 'In Search of Mission: Reflections on "Melbourne" and "Pattaya" '. In *Miss* Vol 9 No 1 (1981) p3—18.

— (1982), 'The Church admidst Cultural Diversity'. In *Miss* Vol 10 No 1 (1982) pp16—28.

BOSHOFF, CWH (1973), 'Die Betekenis van die Swart Teologie vir die Kerk en Sending in Suid-Afrika: Die Swart Teologie as Bevrydingsbeweging'. In *NGTT* Vol 14 No 1 (1973) pp5—20.

— (1980), *Swart teologie: van Amerika tot in Suid-Afrika*. Transvaal: NG Boekhandel 1980.

— (1981a), 'Christ in Black Theology'. In *Miss* Vol 9 No 3 (1981) pp107—125.

— (1981b), 'Christ in Black Theology in a South African Context'. (Paper read at the South African Missiological Society Annual Congress, Potchefstroom, 1981). MS 20pp.

BOTHA, D (1980), 'Church and Kingdom in South Africa: Dutch Reformed Perspective'. In Nash (1980) pp64—84.

BOWERS, Paul (1980), 'Evangelical Theology in Africa: Byang Kato's Legacy'. In *Ev RT* Vol 5 No 1 (1981) pp35—39. (Reprinted from *Trinity Journal* 1, 1980).

BRENEMEN, Mervin (1974), 'The Use of the Exodus in Theology'. In *Th FB* Vol 3 (1974) pp5—9.

BROWN, Colin (ed) (1975) *Dictionary of New Testament Theology*. Exeter: Paternoster Press 1975.

BROWN, E (1973), 'The Necessity of a "Black" South African Church History'. In Becken (1973) pp76—116.

BRYANT, Robert H (1975), 'Towards a Contextualist Theology in Southern Africa'. In *JTSA* Vol 11 (1975) pp11—19.

BUTHELEZI, Manas (1973a), 'Christianity in SA'. In *Pro V* 15 June 1973, pp4—6.

— (1973b), 'African Theology and Black Theology: A Search for a Theological Method'. In Becken (1973) pp18—24.

— (1973c), 'Change in the Church'. In *SAO* August 1973 pp128—130. Also in Anderson & Stransky (1976), pp195—204.

— (1973d), 'Six Theses: Theological Problems of Evangelism in the South African Context'. In *JTSA* Vol 3 (1973) pp55—56.

— (1974a), 'An African Theology or a Black Theology?' In Moore (1974) pp29—35.

— (1974b), 'Theological Grounds for an Ethic of Hope'. In Moore (1974) pp147—156.

— (1974c), 'The Theological Meaning of True Humanity'. In Moore (1974) pp93—103.

— (1974d), 'The Christian Institute and Black South Africa'. In *SAO* October 1974 pp162—164.

— (1974e), 'The Relevance of Black Theology' (Paper read at Swakopmund, August, 1974) MS 5pp. In *SAO* December 1974 pp198—199. Also in AACC (All Africa Conference of Churches) Bulletin Vol 9 No 2 (1976?) pp34—39.

— (1975), 'Black Theology and Le Grange-Schlebusch Commission'. In *Pro V* October 1975 pp4—6.

— (1976), 'The Christian Presence in Today's South Africa'. In *JTSA* Vol 16 (1977) pp5—8.

— (1977), 'Towards a Biblical Faith in South African Society'. In *JTSA* Vol 19 (1977) pp55—58.

— (1978), 'Mutual Acceptance from a Black Perspective'. In *JTSA* Vol 23 (1978) pp71—76.

— (1979), 'Violence and the Cross in South Africa Today'. In *JTSA* Vol 29

(1979) pp51—55.

BUTI, Sam (1976), 'Die NG Kerk in Afrika'. In *T Via* Vol 4 No 1 (April 1976) pp90—97.

— (1978a), 'Race Conflict'. In Cassidy & Verlinden (1978), pp388—389.

— (1978b), 'The Acid Test' (Report on a Sermon preached at Crossroads). In *SAO* August 1978 pp114—115.

— (1978c), 'What is Black Theology?' In Cassidy & Verlinden (1978) pp228—231.

— (1979), 'Shadows of death and the future hope of South Africa'. In Nash (1979) pp11—15.

— (1980), 'Crosscurrents and Crossroads in the South African Scene and the Kingdom of God'. In Nash (1980) pp7—10.

— (1983), 'Transracial Communication', In *Miss* Vol 11 No 3 (1983) pp113—123.

CARSON, DA (1981), 'Hermeneutics: A Brief Assessment of Some Recent Trends'. In *Ev RT* Vol 5 No 1 (1981) pp8—25.

CASSIDY, Michael & VERLINDEN, Luc (1978), *Facing the New Challenges: The Message of PACLA (Pan African Christian Leadership Assembly)*. Kisumu, Kenya: Evangel Publishing House 1978).

CASSIDY, Richard J (1978), *Jesus, Politics and Society*. Maryknoll, NY: Orbis 1978.

CLEAGE, Albert B Jr (1968), *The Black Messiah*. New York: Sheed & Ward 1968.

CONE, James H (1969), *Black Theology and Black Power*. New York: Seabury Press 1969.

— (1970), *A Black Theology of Liberation*. Philadelphia: Lippincourt 1970.

— (1972), *God of the Oppressed*. 2nd edition; (1st edition New York: Seabury Press 1972); London: SPCK 1977.

— (1974), 'Black Theology and Black Liberation'. In Moore (1974) p48—57.

COSTAS, Orlando E (1964), 'Evangelism and the Gospel of Salvation'. In *IRM* Vol 63 (1964) pp24—37.

CRAFFORD, Dion (1973), 'Swart Teologie in die Ned Geref Kerk in Afrika'. In *NGTT* Vol 14 No 1 (1973) pp36—47.

CRIMM, K (ed) (1976), *The Interpreter's Dictionary of the Bible. Supplementary Volume*. Nashville: Abingdon 1976.

DANEEL, ML (1983), 'Communication and Liberation in African Independent Churches'. In *Miss* Vol 11 No2 (1983), pp57-—93.

DAVENPORT, TRH (1977), *South Africa: A Modern History*. Johannesburg: Macmillan 1977.

DAVIES, John (1968?), *A Biblical Commentary on "The Message to the People of South Africa"*. Johannesburg: CI 1968.

DAVIS, Walter T (1980), 'Competing Views of the Kingdom of God in Africa'. In *Ecu R* Vol 32 (1980) pp115—128.

de GRUCHY, John W & de VILLIERS, WB (eds) (1968), *The Message in Perspective: A Book about "A Message to the People in South Africa".* Johannesburg: SACC 1968.

de GRUCHY, John W (1978), 'Miquez Bonino on Latin American Liberation Theology'. In *JTSA* Vol 22 (1978) pp62—66.

— (1979), *The Church Struggle in South Africa.* 2nd edition; (1st edition Grand Rapids: Eerdmans 1979); Cape Town: David Philip 1979.

de KLERK, WA (1975), *The Puritans in Africa: A Story of Afrikanerdom.* Harmondsworth, Middlesex: Penguin 1975.

DEIST, F (1977), 'The Exodus Motif in the Old Testament and the Theology of Liberation'. In *Miss* Vol 5 No 2 (1977) pp58—69.

DICKSON, Kwesi A & ELLINGWORTH, Paul (eds) (1969), *Biblical Revelation and African Beliefs.* London: Lutterworth Press 1969.

DICKSON, Kwesi A (1974), 'Towards a *Theologia Africana*'. In Glasswell & Fasholé-Luke (1974) pp198—208.

DUMMETT, M (1979), *Catholicism and the World Order: Some Reflections on the 1978 Reith Lectures.* London: Catholic Institute for International Relations 1979.

DUNSTAN, Jo (1979), 'A South African Dramatist's Critical Look at Calvinism: Adam Small's "The Orange Earth" '. In *JTSA* Vol 27 (1979) pp20—25.

DURAND, JJF (1975), 'Black Theology in a SA Context'. In *Theological Bulletin* Vol 3 No 2 (May 1975) pp1—8.

— (1978) 'Bible and Race: The Problem of Hermeneutics'. In *JTSA* Vol 24 (1978) pp3—11.

DWANE, Sigqibo (1977), 'Christology in the Third World'. In *JTSA* Vol 21 (1977) pp3—12.

— (1980), 'Black Christianity in Kingdom Perspective'. In Nash (1980) pp30—39.

— (1981), 'Christology and Liberation'. In *JTSA* Vol 35 (1981) pp29—37.

— (1982), 'In Search of an African Contribution to a Contemporary Confession of Christian Faith'. In *JTSA* Vol 38 (1982) pp19—25.

ELLIS, Ieuan P (1974), 'In Defense of Early North African Christianity'. In Glasswell & Fasholé-Luke (1974) pp157—165.

ENGELBRECHT, Ben (1978), *God en die Politiek.* Durban: Butterworth 1978.

— (1980a), 'The Indwelling of the Holy Spirit: An Evaluation of Contemporary Pneumatology 1'. In *JTSA* Vol 30 (1980) pp19—33.

—(1980b), 'The Indwelling of the Holy Spirit. An Evaluation of Contemporary Pneumatology 2'. In *JTSA* Vol 31 (1980) pp36—45.

— (1982), *Ter wille van hierdie wêreld: Politiek en Christelike Heilsbelewing in Suid-Afrika*. Cape Town: Tafelberg 1982.

ETHERINGTON, NA (1979), 'The Historical Sociology of Independent Churches in South East Africa'. In *JRA* Vol 10 No 2 (1979) pp108—126.

FASHOLÉ-LUKE, Edward W (1974a), 'What is African Christian Theology?' In *Com Via* Vol 17 (1974) pp97—102.

— (1974b), 'Ancestor Veneration and the Communion of Saints'. In Glasswell & Fasholé-Luke (1974) pp209—221.

— (1976), 'The Quest for African Christian Theologies'. In Anderson & Stransky (1976) pp136—150.

FASHOLÉ-LUKE, Edward W *et al* (eds) (1978), *Christianity in Independent Africa*. London: Rex Collings 1978.

FIORENZA, Francis P (1974), 'Latin American Liberation Theology', In *Interpretation* Vol 28 (1974) pp441—457.

FRANCE, Dick (1979), 'Questions Concerning the Future of African Christianity'. In *Ev RT* Vol 3 No 1 (1979) pp27—26.

FURLONG, Patrick J (1983), 'Catholic Initiatives in the Africanization of Christianity'. In *JTSA* Vol 43 (1983) pp25—34.

GABA, Christian R (1978), 'Man's Salvation: Its Nature and Meaning in African Traditional Religion'. In Fasholé-Luke *et al* (1978) pp389—401.

GERHART, Gail (1978), *Black Power in South Africa: The Evolution of an Ideology*. Los Angeles, London: Univ of California Press 1978.

GERWEL, CJ (1973), 'Black Power: SA'. In *SAO* July 1973, pp119—120.

GEYSER, AS *et al* (eds) (1961), *Delayed Action*. Pretoria: NG Boekhandel 1961.

GIBELLINI, Rosino (ed) (1975), *Frontiers of Theology in Latin America*. ET (Spanish original published in Rome 1975) London: SCM 1980.

GLASSWELL, Mark E & FASOLÉ-LUKE, Edward W (eds) (1974), *New Testament Christianity for Africa and the World: Essays in Honour of Harry Sawyerr*. London: SPCK 1974.

GOBA, Bonganjalo, 'The Church and the Problem of Racism in South Africa: A Black Christian Perspective'. In *Consultation of Church Representatives on Racism in South Africa (SACC)* (nd)pp15—23.

— (1974), 'Corporate Personality: Ancient Israel and Africa'. In Moore (1974) pp65—73.

— (1978), 'The Task of Black Theological Education in South Africa'. In *JTSA* Vol 22 (1978) pp19—30.

— (1979), 'An African Christian Theology: Towards a Tentative Methodology from a South Africa Perspective'. In *JTSA* Vol 26 (1979) pp3—12.

— (1980), 'Doing Theology in South Africa'. In *JTSA* Vol 31 (1980) pp23—35.

— (1981), 'Towards a "Black" Ecclesiology'. In *Miss* Vol 9 No 2 (1981) pp47—58.

— (1982), 'The Role of the Urban Church: A Black South African Perspective'. In *JTSA* Vol 38 (1982) pp26—33.

GOVENDER, Shun (1979), 'Reconciling Mission in the Contemporary South African Situation of Cultural Pluralism and Indentity. In *Miss* Vol 7 No 2 (August 1979) pp78—89.

GQUBULE, Simon (1974), 'What is Black Theology?'. In *JTSA* Vol 8 (1974) pp16—23.

— (1979), 'Can Each Church Remain United?'. In Nash (1979), pp26—30.

GROTH, Siegfried (1972), 'The Condemnation of Apartheid by the Churches in South West Africa'. In *IRM* Vol 61 (1972) pp183—193.

GUTIERREZ, Gustavo (1971), *A Theology of Liberation.* ET (Spanish original published in Lima, 1971) London: SCM 1974.

HASELBARTH, Hans (1975), 'The Relevance of Black Theology for Independent Africa'. (Paper read at Jos, Nigeria, September 1975). MS 19pp.

HASTINGS, Adrian (1975), 'On the Nature of African Theology'. (Paper for discussion at Jos, Nigeria, 3 September 1975). MS 5pp.

— (1976), *African Theology.* London: Geoffrey Chapman, 1976.

— (1979), *A History of African Christianity 1950—1975.* Cambridge: CUP 1979.

HERBSTEIN, Denis (1978), *White Man, We Want to Talk to You.* Harmondsworth, Middlesex: Penguin 1978.

HEXHAM, Irving (1980), 'Christianity and Apartheid: Introductory Bibliography'. In *JTSA* Vol 32 (1980) pp39—59.

HILL, Edmund (1974), 'The Impenitent Ostrich'. In *SAO* March 1974 pp41—43.

HINCHLIFF, Peter (1968), *The Church in South Africa.* London SPCK 1968.

HINWOOD, Bonaventura (1975a), 'Revelation in Non-Christian Religions 1'. In *JTSA* Vol 11 (1975) pp55—70.

— (1975b), 'Revelation in Non-Christian Religions 2'. In *JTSA* Vol 13 (1975) pp61—73.

HOFMEYER, JM (1974), 'Black Students and the Afrikaans Churches'. In *Miss* Vol 2 No 3 (1974) pp172—178.

HOPE, Marjorie & YOUNG, James (1981), *The South African Churches in a Revolutionary Situation.* Maryknoll, NY: Orbis 1981.

HUDDLESTON, Trevor (1956), *Naught for your Comfort.* London: Collins 1956.

HUNDLEY, Raymond C (1981a), 'Liberationist Themes in Selected Documents of the World Council of Churches (1968—1975)'. MS 14pp.

— (1981b), 'The Antecedents of the World Council of Churches and the Theology of Liberation'. MS 8pp.

— (1981c), 'Introduction to Latin American Liberation Theology.' (Paper presented to the St John's College Theological Society, Cambridge, 3 November 1981). MS 13pp.

IDOWU, E Bolaji (1962), *Olódùmarè: God in Yoruba Belief*. London: Longmans 1962.

— (1973), *African Traditional Religion: A Definition*. London: SCM 1973.

JOHANSON, Brian (1974), *Human Rights in South Africa*. Johannesburg: SACC 1974.

— (1975), 'Race, Mission and Ecumenism: Reflections of the Landman Report'. In *JTSA* Vol 10 (1975), pp51—61.

JONES, David C (1978) 'Who are the Poor?' In *Ev RT* Vol 2 No 1 (1978), pp215—226.

KANE-BERMAN, John (1978), *Soweto: Black Revolt, White Reaction*. Johannesburg: Ravan Press 1978.

KARIS, Thomas & CARTER, GM (eds) (1972), *From Protest to Challenge: A Documentary History of African Politics in South Africa 1882—1964 Vol 1—4*. Stanford, California: Stanford UP 1972.

KATO, Byang H (1976), 'An Evaluation of Black Theology'. In *Bib Sacra* Vol 133 (1976) pp243—255.

— (1977), 'Black Theology and African Theology'. In *Ev RT* Vol 1 (1977) pp35—48.

— (1979), 'Christianity as an African Religion'. In *Ev RT* Vol 4 No 1 (1980) pp31—39. (Reprinted from *Perception* May 1979).

KECK, LE (1976), 'Poor'. In Crimm (1976).

KEE, Alistair (ed) (1974), *A Reader in Political Theology*. London: SCM 1974.

KHOAPA, Bennie A (1972), 'Black Consciousness'. In *SAO* June/July 1972 pp100—102.

KIERNAN, James (1980), 'Zionist Communion'. In *JRA* Vol 11 No 2 (1980) pp124—136.

KING, Coretta S (1969), *My Life with Martin Luther King Jnr* London: Hodder & Stoughton 1969.

KING, Martin Luther (1963), *Strength to Love*. London: Collins 1963.

— (1969), *Chaos or Community?* Harmondsworth, Middlesex: Penguin 1969.

KIRK, J Andrew (1976), 'Beyond Capitalism and Marxism: Dialogue with a Dialogue'. In *Th FB* Vol 2 (1976) pp26—38.

— (1977), 'The Use of the Bible in Interpreting Salvation Today: An Evangelical Perspective'. In *Ev RT* Vol 1 (1977) pp1—20.

— (1978), 'The Gospel we Preach and South Africa Today'. In *T Via* Vol 6 No 1 (July 1978) pp30—42.

—(1979a), *Liberation Theology: An Evangelical View from the Third World*. London: Marshall, Morgan & Scott 1979.

— (1979b), 'Christian Witness and the Challenge of Marxism'. In Nash (1979) pp31—38.

— (1979c), 'Marxism and the Church in Latin America'. In *Ev Rt* Vol 3 No 1 (1979) pp107—118.

— (1980a), *Theology Encounters Revolution*. Leicester: Inter-Varsity Press 1980.

— (1980b), 'The Kingdom, the Church and a Distressed World'. In *Ev R T* Vol 5 No 1 (1981) pp74—93. (Reprinted from *Churchmen* Vol 94 No 2, 1980.)

KLEINSCHMIDT, H (ed) (1972), *White Liberation*. Johannesburg: Ravan Press 1972.

KÖNIG, Adrio (1978), 'Die Roeping van die Kerk in die Heersende Politieke en Ekonomiese Probleme in Suid-Afrika'. In *T Via* Vol 6 No 1 (July 1978) pp43—53.

KOTZE, DJ (1977), 'Swartbewustheid, Swart Teologie en Swart Mag'. In *Tydskrif vir Geesteswetenskap* Vol 17 (1977) pp220—233.

KRAFT, Charles H (1980), *Christianity in Culture*, Maryknoll, NY: Orbis Books 1980.

KRUGER, JS (1979), 'Theology as a Response to Social Change: A Case Study'. In *Miss* Vol 7 No 1 (1979) pp17—30.

KUREWA, JW Zvomunondita (1975), 'The Meaning of African Theology'. In *JTSA* Vol 11 (1975) pp32—42.

— (1980), 'Who do you say that I am?'. In *IRM* Vol 69 (1980) pp182—188.

LAMPRECHT, John A (1975), 'Commending Christ in a Multi-racial Society'. In *JTSA* Vol 11 (1975) pp20—31.

LEDIGA, SP (1971), 'The Concept is an Old One — Nothing New!: Black Consciousness and Black Power'. (Paper read at the National Seminar on Black Theology, Roodepoort, March 1971). MS 3pp.

— (1973), 'A Relevant Theology for Africa: A Critical Evaluation of Previous Attempts'. In Becken (1973), pp25—33.

LOEWEN, Jacob A (1976), 'Mission Churches, Independent Churches, and Felt Needs in Africa'. In *Miss* Vol 4 No 4 (1976), pp404—425.

LONG, Charles H (1975), 'Structural Similarities and Dissimilarities in Black and African Theologies', In *Journal of Religious Thought* Vol 32 No 2 (1975) pp9—24.

LUNGU, MT (1982) 'Xhosa Ancestor Veneration and the Communion of Saints'. MTh dissertation, UNISA, 1982.

LUTHULI, Albert (1962), *Let My People Go*. London: Collins 1962.

MABONA, Mongameli (1974), 'Black People and White Worship'. In Moore (1974) pp104—108.

MAIMELA, Simon S (1981a), 'Man in "White" Theology'. In *Miss* Vol 9 No 2 (1981) pp64—77.

— (1981b), 'The Atonement in the Context of Liberation Theology'. In *SAO*

December 1981 pp183—186. (Reprinted in *JTSA* Vol 39 (1982) pp45—54.)

— (1982), 'Towards a Theology of Humanization'. In *JTSA* Vol 41   (1982) pp58—65.

MAKHATHINI, DDL (1973), 'Black Theology 1 & 2'. In Becken (1973) pp8—17.

— (1974), 'Black Theology — What is it?' (Paper read to the Christian Academy and the Witwatersrand Council of Churches, 25 May 1974.) MS 4pp.

MAKHAYE, MM (1973), 'Sickness and Healing in African Perspective, with Application to Counselling'. In Becken (1973) pp158—162.

MANGANYI, NC (1973), *Being Black in the World*. Johannesburg: Sprocas/Ravan 1973.

MANNIKAM, E (1973), 'Mixed Worship is Necessary'. In *Pro V* 15 May 1973 pp4—8.

MARSHALL, I Howard (ed) (1977), *New Testament Interpretation*. Exeter: Paternoster 1977.

MARSHALL, I Howard (1978), *The Gospel of Luke*. Exeter: Paternoster 1978.

MATTHEWS, James (1974), 'Christians'. In Moore (1974) p64.

MBITI, John S (1970a), *Concepts of God in Africa*. London: SPCK 1970.

— (1970b), 'The Future of Christianity in Africa (1970—2000)'. In *Com Via* Vol 13 (1970) pp19—38.

— (1977), 'Christianity and African Culture'. In *JTSA* Vol 20 (1977) pp26—40.

— (1979a), 'The Biblical Basis for Present Trends in African Theology'. In Appiah-Kubi & Torres (1979) pp83—95.

— (1979b), 'An African Views American Black Theology'. In Wilmore & Cone (1979) pp477—481.

MEIRING, PGJ (1974), 'Die Agtergrond van Swart Teologie in Afrika en Suid-Afrika'. In *Bulletin* Vol 6 (1974) pp1—15.

METZ, Rene & SCHLICK, Jean (ed) (1978), *Liberation Theology and the Message of Salvation (Papers of the Fourth Cerdic Colloquium, Strasbourg, May 10—12, 1973)*. Pittsburg: Pickwick Press 1978.

MGOJO, Elliot KM (1977), 'Prolegomenon to the Study of Black Theology'. In *JTSA* Vol 21 (1977) pp25—32.

MIGUEZ-BONINO, José (1976), 'Five Theses towards an Understanding of· the 'Theology of Liberation'' '. In *Exp T* Vol 87 No 7 (1976) pp196—200.

MOKOENA, Aubrey Dundubele (1975), 'African Culture'. In *Pro V* May 1977 pp10—11.

MOLTMANN, J & METZ, JB *et al* (1974), *Religion and Political Society*. New York: Harper & Row 1974.

MOODIE, T Dunbar (1975), *The Rise of Afrikanerdom: Power, Apartheid and Afrikaner Civil Religion.* London: Univ of California Press 1975.

MOORE, Basil (1971), 'Towards a Black Theology'. (Paper read at the Roodepoort Seminar on Black Theology, March 1971?) MS 25pp.

— (ed) (1973), *The Challenge of Black Theology in South Africa.* 2nd edition; (1st edition London: Hurst 1973 — almost identical with Motlhabi, Johannesburg: Ravan 1972) Atlanta, Georgia: John Knox Press 1974.

— (1974), 'What is Black Theology?' In Moore (1974) pp1—10.

MOSALA, Jerry (1983a), 'African Traditional Beliefs and Christianity'. In *JTSA* Vol 43 (1983) pp15—24.

— (1983b), 'Liberation Theology'. In *Link, TEEC News* Vol 14 August 1983.

MOSOTHOANE, EK (1973), 'The Message of the New Testament seen in African Perspective'. In Becken (1973) pp55—67.

— (1977), 'The Liberation of Peoples in the New Testament?' In *Miss* Vol 5 No 2 (1977) pp70—80.

— (1979), 'The Use of Scripture in Black Theology'. In Vorster (1979) pp28—37.

— (1981), 'Towards a Theology for South Africa'. In *Miss* Vol 9 No 3 (1981) pp98—107.

MOTLHABI, Mokgethi (ed) (1972), *Essays in Black Theology.* Johannesburg: Ravan Press 1972.

MOTLHABI, Mokgethi (1974a), 'Black Theology: A Personal View'. In Moore (1974) pp74—80.

— (1974b), 'Black Theology and Authority'. In Moore (1974) pp119—129.

MPHAHLELE, Ezekiel (1977), 'South Africa: Two Communities and the Struggle for a Birthright'. In *JAS* Vol 4 No 1 (1977) pp21—50.

MPUNZI, Ananias (1974), 'Black Theology as Liberation Theology'. In Moore (1974) pp 130—140.

MSHANA, Eliewaha E (1972), 'The Challenge of Black Theology and African Theology'. In *Africa Theological Journal* Vol 5 December 1972 pp19—30.

NASH, M (ed) (1979), *The Church and the Alternative Society: Papers and Resolutions of the Eleventh Conference of the SACC.* Johannesburg: SACC 1979.

— (1980), *Your Kingdom Come: Papers and Resolutions of the Twelfth Conference of the SACC.* Johannesburg: SACC 1980.

NOLAN, Albert (1976), *Jesus before Christianity: The Gospel of Liberation.* London: Darton, Longman & Todd 1976.

NORMAN, Edward (1979), *Christianity and the World Order.* Oxford: OUP 1979.

— (1981), *Christianity in the Southern Hemisphere.* Oxford: Clarendon Press 1981.

NTOULA, Revelation (1976), 'South Africa's Black "Daughter" Churches

Fight for Change'. In *SAO* September 1976 p142.

NTWASA, Sabelo (1971), 'A Personal Report and Assessment of the *National Seminar on Black Theology*'. (Paper read at the Roodepoort Seminar on Black Theology, March 1971). MS 6pp.

NTWASA, Sabelo & MOORE, Basil (1974a), 'The Concept of God in Black Theology'. In Moore (1974) pp18—28.

NTWASA, Sebelo (1974b), 'The Concept of the Church in Black Theology'. In Moore (1974) pp109—118.

— (1974c), 'The Training of Black Ministers Today'. In Moore (1974) pp141—161.

NÜRNBERGER, Klaus (1972), 'Comment [on Missiological Institute's Consultation, September 1972]'. In *JTSA* Vol 1 (1972) pp59—63.

— (1979), 'Christian Witness and Economic Discrepancies'. In *JTSA* Vol 29 (1979) pp72—77.

NUÑEZ, Emilio A (1977), 'The Theology of Liberation in Latin America'. In *Bib Sacra* (1977) pp343—356.

NXUMALO, Jabulani A (1979), 'Church as Mission'. In *JTSA* Vol 26 (1979) pp38—49.

— (1980), 'Christ and Ancestors in the African World: A Pastoral Consideration'. In *JTSA* Vol 32 (1980) pp3—21.

— (1981a), 'A Response to Sigqibo Dwane'. In *JTSA* Vol 35 (1981) pp38—41.

— (1981b), 'The Church from a Black Perspective: A Response to Bonganjalo Goba'. In *Miss* Vol 9 No 2 (1981) pp59—64.

O'BRIEN GELDENHUYS, FE (1976), 'The Church's Role in Liberation'. In Thomas (1976) pp26—46.

OLIVER, Roland (1956), *How Christian is Africa?'* London: Highway Press 1956.

OMOYAJOWO, Akin J (1974), 'An African Expression of Christianity'. In Moore (1974) pp81—92.

OOSTHUISEN, GC (1968), *Post-Christianity in Africa.* London: C Hurst & Co 1968.

PADILLA, René (1981), 'The Interpreted Word: Reflections on Contextual Hermeneutics'. In *Themelios* Vol 7 (1981), pp18—23.

PARRINDER, Geoffrey (1954), *African Traditional Religion.* London: Hutchinson University Library 1954.

PATO, Luke LL (1980), 'The Communion of Saints and Ancestor Veneration: A Study of the Concept "Communion of Saints" with Special Reference to the South African Religious Experience'. MA Diss. Manitoba University, Canada 1980. MS 133pp.

PEEL, JDY (1978), 'The Christianization of African Society: Some possible models'. In Fasholé-Luke *et al* (1978) pp443—454.

PEREZ, Pablo (1974), 'Liberationistic Roots in Latin America'. In *Th FB* Vol 3 (1974) pp8—12.

PITYANA, Nyameko (1974), 'What is Black Consciousness?' In Moore (1974) pp58—63.

POBEE, John S (1979), *Toward an African Theology*. Nashville: Abingdon 1979.

PRETORIUS, Hennie L (1977), 'Wit/Swart Bevrydingsteologie in Suid-Afrika'. In *NGTT* Vol 18 No 4 (1977) pp343—352.

— (1981), 'White South African Ecclesiology'. In *Miss* Vol 9 No 1 (1981) pp18—32.

RANDALL, Peter (ed) (1972a), *Power Privilege and Poverty: Report of the Spro-cas Economics Commission*. Johannesburg: Spro-Cas 1972.

— (1972b), *Apartheid and the Church: Report of the Spro-cas Church Commission* Johannesburg: Spro-cas 1972.

REGEHR, Ernie (1979), *Perceptions of Apartheid: The Churches and Political Change in South Africa*. Kitchener, Ontario: Between the Lines 1979.

ROBERTS, J Deotis (1974), *A Black Political Theology*. Philadelphia: Westminster Press 1974.

ROOY, Sidney H (1981), 'Reflections on the Theology of Liberation'. In *The Reformed Journal* Vol 31 No 2 (1981) pp7—12.

ROUX, Edward (1948), *Time Longer than Rope: The Black Man's Struggle for Freedom in South Africa*. 2nd edition; (1st edition 1948); Madison & London: Univerity of Wisconsin 1964.

SAAYMAN, Willem (1979), 'A few Aspects of the Policy of Separate Churches'. In *JTSA* Vol 26 (1979) pp50—55.

SALLEY, C & BEHM, R (1970), *Your God is Too White*. Hertfordshire: Lion 1970.

SCHROTENBOER, Paul G (1978), 'The Bible in the World Council of Churches'. In *Ev RT* Vol 2 No 1 (1978) pp162—180.

SEBIDI, Lebamang, J (1977), 'Encounter of African Religion with Christianity'. In *Pro V* May 1977 pp11—14.

SERFONTEIN, JHP (1982), *Apartheid, Change and the NG Kerk*. Johannesburg: Taurus 1982.

SEROTE, SE (1973), 'Meaningful Christian Worship for Africa'. In Becken (1973) pp148—154.

SETILOANE, Gabriel M (1973a), *The Image of God Amongst the Sotho-Tswana*. Rotterdam: AA Balkema 1976.

— (1973b), 'Modimo: God Among the Sotho-Tswana'. In *JTSA* Vol 4 (1973) pp4—17.

— (1978), 'How the Traditional World-View Persists in the Christianity of the Sotho-Tswana'. In Fasholé-Luke (1978) pp402—412.

— (1980), 'Theological Trends in Africa'. In *Miss* Vol 8 No 2 (August 1980) pp47—53.

SHORTER, Aylward (1973), *African Culture and the Christian Church*. London: Geoffrey Chapman 1973.

SHUUYA, IK, (1973), 'The Encounter Between the New Testament and African Traditional Concepts'. In Becken (1973), pp47—54.

SIDER, Ronald J (1978), 'Evangelism, Salvation and Social Justice'. In *Ev RT* Vol 2 No 1 (1978) pp70—88.

SIKAKANE, Enos (1974), 'The Need for Black Theology'. In *Pro V* April 1974 pp20—23.

SIMPSON, Theodore (1974) 'Black Theology — and White'. In *Pro V* March 1974 pp16—20.

SLABBERT, J van Zyl & WELSH, David (1979), *South Africa's Options — Strategies for Sharing Power*. Cape Town: David Philip 1979.

SMALL, Adam (1974), 'Blackness versus Nihilism: Black Racism Rejected'. In Moore (1974) pp11—17.

SMIT, AJC (1972), 'Swart Teologie'. In *Die Kerkbode* 26 January 1972 pp106—108.

SMIT, JH (1981), ' "White" Ecclesiology — A Response to HL Pretorius'. In *Miss* Vol 9 No 1 (1981) pp33—34.

SMITH, Nico J, O'BRIEN GELDENHUYS, FE & MEIRING, Piet (eds) (1981), *Storm Kompas*. Cape Town: Tafelberg 1981.

SMITH, PES (1973), 'Swart Teologie en die Sending van die Kerk'. In *NGTT* Vol 14 No 1 (1973) pp21—35.

STEYN, MT (ed) (1982), *Report on the Commission of Inquiry into the Mass Media, Vols 1—3*. Pretoria: Government Printer? 1982.

SUNDERMEIER, Theo (ed) (1975), *Church and Nationalism in South Africa*. Johannesburg: Ravan Press 1975.

SUNDKLER, Bengt GM (1960), *The Christian Ministry in Africa*. London: SCM 1960.

— (1961), *Bantu Prophets in South Africa*. Oxford : OUP 1961.

— (1976), *Zulu, Zion, and some Swazi Zionists*. Uppsala: Gleerups 1976.

— (1978), 'Worship and Spirituality'. In Fasholé-Luke *et al* (1978) pp545—553.

SWITZER, Les (1983), 'Reflections on the Mission Press in South Africa in the 19th and early 20th Centuries'. In *JTSA* Vol 43 (1973) pp5—14.

THEBEHALI, David (1971), 'Has Christianity any Relevance for and Future among Black People in South Africa?' (Paper read at the Roodepoort Seminar on Black Theology, March 1971.) MS 5pp.

THISELTON, AC (1977), 'The New Hermeneutic'. In Marshall (1977) pp308—333.

— (1980), *The Two Horizons*. Exeter: Paternoster Press 1980.

THOAHLANE, T (ed) (1975), *Black Renaissance*. Johannesburg: Ravan 1975.

THOMAS, D (ed) (1976), *Liberation: Papers and Resolutions for the Eighth National Conference of the SACC*. Johannesburg: SACC 1976.

TIENOU, Tite (1979), 'Christianity and African Culture: A Review'. In *Ev RT* Vol 3 No 2 (1979) pp198—205.

— (1981), 'Threats & Dangers in the Theological Task in Africa'. In *Ev RT* Vol 5 No 1 (1981) pp40—47.

TURNER, Harold W (1969), 'The Place of Independent Religious Movements in the Modernization of Africa'. In *JRA* Vol 2 No 1 (1969) pp43—63.

— (1975), 'Survey Article: The Study of New Religious Movements in Africa, 1968—1975'. In *Religion* August 1975 pp88—98.

— (1978), 'Patterns of Ministry and Structure within Independent Churches'. In Fasholé-Luke *et al* (1978) pp44—59.

— (1980), 'African Religious Research — New Studies of New Movements'. In *JRA* Vol 11 No 2 (1980), pp137—153.

— (1983a), 'Shona and/or Christian'. In *Miss* Vol 11 No 1 (1983) pp11—16.

— (1983b), 'A Further Frontier for Missions: A General Introduction to New Religious Movements in Primal Societies'. In *Miss* Vol 11 No 3 (1983) pp103—112.

TUTU, Desmond (1971), 'God — Black or White?'. In *Ministry* Vol 11 No 4 (1971) pp111—115.

— (1972), 'Some African Insights and the Old Testament'. In *JTSA* Vol 1 (1972) pp16—22.

— (1975), 'Black Theology/African Theology — Soul Mates or Antagonists?'. In Wilmore & Cone (1979), pp483—491. (First published in the *Journal of Religious Thought* Vol 32 No 2 1975 pp25—33.)

— (1976a), 'God-Given Dignity and the Quest for Liberation in the Light of the South African Dilemma'. In Thomas (1976) pp53—59.

— (1976b), 'God and Nation in the Perspective of Black Theology'. In *JTSA* Vol 15 (1976) pp5—11.

— (1977), 'God Intervening in Human Affairs'. In *Miss* Vol 5 No 2 (1977) pp111—117.

— (1978), 'Whither African Theology?' In Fasholé-Luke *et al* (1978) pp364—369.

— (1979a), 'Called to Unity and Fellowship'. In Nash (1979) pp16—25.

— (1979b), 'The Theology of Liberation in Africa'. In Appiah-Kubi & Torres (1979) pp162—168.

van der ROSS, RE (1975), 'Black Power'. In *SAO* November 1975 pp177—178.

van ROOY, JA (1981), 'The Image of Man in White Theology: Calvinist,

Biblical or Self-centred?' In *Miss* Vol 9 No 2 (1981) pp78—85.

VERKUYL, J (1970), *The Message of Liberation in our Age.'* Grand Rapids: Eerdmans 1970.

— (1972), 'Theological Reflections on Apartheid'. In *SAO* June/July 1972 p104.

— (1973), *Break Down the Walls: A Christian Cry for Racial Justice.* Grand Rapids: Eerdmans 1973.

VERRYN, TD (1973), 'Rites of Passage'. In Becken (1973), pp139—147.

VILLA-VICENCIO, Charles (1976), 'Theology and Politics in South Africa: An Examination of Some Theological Writing in South Africa'. In *JTSA* Vol 17 (1976) pp25—34.

— (1981), 'The Use of Scripture in Theology: Towards a Conceptual Hermeneutic'. In *JTSA* Vol 37 (1981) pp3—12.

— (1982), 'Where Faith and Ideology Meet: The Political Task of Theology'. In *JTSA* Vol 41 (1982) pp78—82.

— (1983), 'Southern Africa Today, Vancouver: A Quest for Reintegration'. In *JTSA* Vol 44 (1983) pp73—78.

VORSTER, WS (ed) (1979), *Scripture and the use of Scripture.* Pretoria: UNISA Press 1979.

VUNDLA, Kathleen (1973), *PQ: The Story of Philip Vundla of South Africa.* Johannesburg: Moral Re-armament 1973.

WA SAID, Dibinga (1971), 'An African Theology of Decolonization'. In *HRT* Vol 64 (1971) pp501—524.

WALLS, Andrew F (1979), 'The Challenge of African Independent Churches'. In *Ev RT* Vol 4 No 2 (1980) pp225—234. (Reprinted from *Occasional Bulletin* April 1979).

— (1982), 'The Gospel as Prisoner and Liberator of Culture'. In *Miss* Vol 10 No 3 (1982) pp93—105.

WALSHE, P (1970), *The Rise of African Nationalism in South Africa.* London: C Hurst & Co 1970.

WEBSTER, John (ed) (1982), *Bishop Desmond Tutu: The Voice of One Crying in the Wilderness.* Oxford: Mowbray 1982.

WELLS, Harold (1981), 'Segundo's Hermeneutical Circle'. In *JTSA* Vol 34 (1981) pp25—31.

WEST, Martin (1975), *Bishops and Prophets in a Black City: African Independent Churches in Soweto, Johannesburg.* Cape Town: David Philip 1975.

WILKENS, Ivor & STRYDOM, Hans (1979), *The Broederbond: The Super-Afrikaners.* 2nd edition; (1st edition London: Paddington 1979); London: Corgi 1980.

WILMORE, Gayraud S (1972), *Black Religion and Black Radicalism.* New York: Doubleday & Anchor Press 1972.

WILMORE, Gayraud S & Cone, James H (eds) (1979), *Black Theology: A Documentary History, 1966—1979,* Maryknoll, NY: Orbis Books 1979.

WILSON, Francis & PERROT, Dominique (eds) (1972), *Outlook on a Century: South Africa 1870—1970.* Johannesburg: Lovedale and Spro-cas 1972.

YODER, John H (1974), 'Exodus and Exile: The Two Faces of Liberation'. In *Miss* Vol 2 No 1 (1974) pp29—41.

— (1979), 'The Spirit of God and the Politics of Man'. In *JTSA* Vol 29 (1979) pp67—71.

ZULU, Alphaeus (1972), *The Dilemma of the Black South African.* Cape Town: UCT Press 1972, 14pp.

— (1973), 'Whither Black Theology?' In *Pro* V March 1973 pp11—13.

b) DOCUMENTS AND REPORTS (in chronological order)

Cottesloe Consultation (The Report of the Consultation among South African Member Churches of the World Council of Churches. Cottesloe, Johannesburg: SACC 1960).

A Message to the People of South Africa (Johannesburg: SACC 1968).

'Swart Teologie' in *Die Kerkbode* (14 April 1971) 508—509.

The Commission of Black Theology, SASO Newsletter (August 1971) 17.

'Swart Teologie' in *Die Sendingblad* (August 1971) 258—261.

Kinshasa Declaration (All African Conference of Churches, 31 October 1971) IRM 61 (1972) 115—116.

Apartheid and the Church, P Randall (ed) (Johannesburg: Spro-cas Report 1972).

'Conference on Black Theology' in *DRC Newsletter* 161 (May 1974).

Findings of the Missiological Institute: Consultation on Church and Nationalism, Umpumulo, September 1974, 1—8.

The Cyara Declaration (Statement by the Students' Christian Movement of South Africa) *Pro* V (July 1976) 12—13.

Liberation: Papers and Resolutions of the Eighth National Conference of the South African Council of Churches. Held at St Peter's Conference Centre, Hammanskraal, July 27—29 1976, (ed) D Thomas (Johannesburg: SACC 1976).

Human Relations in the South African Scene in the Light of Scripture (Cape Town: DRC Publishers, General Synod of the DRC (NGK): *Ras. Volk en Nasie en Volkereverhoudinge in die Lig van die Skrif,* October 1974.

Consultation of Church Representatives on Racism in South Africa (Johannesburg: SACC, nd).

The Church and the Alternative Society: Papers and Resolutions of the

Eleventh Conference of the South African Council of Churches, Hammanskraal (Johannesburg: SACC 1979).

Your Kingdom Come: Papers and Resolutions of the Twelfth National Conference of the South African Council of Churches, Hammanskraal, May 5—8 1980, (ed) M Nash (Johannesburg: SACC 1980).

The Koinonia Declaration (Produced in November 1977 by a group of concerned South African Calvinists from Potchefstroom and a study group 'The Loft', in Germiston) *JTSA* 24 (1978) 58—64.

The Christian Witness in Society (A Response to the Koinonia Declaration by Members of the Transkei Region of the SA Missiological Society) *JTSA* 30 (1980) 68—72.

World Council of Churches' Statements and Actions on Racism 1948—1979 (ed) Ans J van der Bent (Geneva: WCC Programme to Combat Racism, 1980).

Association for Christian Students of Southern Africa (Declaration on South African Society, nd) 1—6.

Students' Christian Association Declaration 1980 (National Students Committee of SCA, March 1981) 1—7.

Index

African culture: 13, 25, 33-38, 44, 46, 112

African Independent Churches (AICs): 10, 12, 30, 43-57, *55n1, n14, n20,* 112-113
establishment of: 1-2, 43-44, 46-48
growth of: 44-48
contribution of: 48-52
and social transformation: 52-55, *57n45*

African National Congress (ANC): 4-5, 7-8, 10, 13*n6,* 60
Freedom Charter: 9
and PAC: 10, 12

African Theology: 14-16, 18, 21, 24-42, *39n1, 40n11,* 44, 101, 104, 111-112
and AICs: 43-57
and socio-political issues: 38-39

African traditional religion: 13, 26-31, 38, 45, 112

Afrikaner civil religion: 66, 94, 106-7*n1,* 109*n52*

Ancestor veneration: 28-33, *57n38*

Apartheid (Separate Development): 9, 11-12, 47, 52, 64, 69*n20,* 74, 78, 83, 85, 94-100

Association for the Educational, Social and Cultural Advancement of the African People of South Africa (ASSECA): 7, 60

Baartman, Ernest: 62, 67, 80

Biko, Steve: 58, 64

Black Consciousness: 39, 58, 68, 70, 100, 104, 113

and racism and integration: 62-65

Black Messiah: 48, *56n13,* 65

Black Power: 17, 66, 80, 100

Black Theology in South Africa: 14, 21, 22*n1,* 44, 58-70, 91*n35,* 114
early form of: 3-12, 68*n2*
and Black Consciousness: 60-62
and violence: 108*n40*
and racism and integration: 62-65
and black nationalism and reconciliation: 65-68
and black liberation: 1, 71-93
reaction to: 100-106, 110-115

Black Theology in United States of America: 16-19, 63, 67, 101-102, 111, 113

Boesak, Allan: 18, 62-63, 65, 67, 72, 75-81, 83, 101

Bosch, David: 28-29, 37, 38, 103-105

Boshoff, CWH: 68*n5,* 100-101, 103

Buthelezi, Manas: 26, 61-65, 67, 79-80, 82

Buti, Sam: 64, 83

Cone, James: 17-18, 21, 59, 65, 71-72, 76-78, 80-81, 100-101

Contextualisation (Indigenisation and Africanisation): 24, 37, 39, 43-44, 74, 90*n12,* 112-113

Cottesloe Consultation: 96

De Gruchy, J: 49, 71, 97, 104, 105

Dwane, S: 77-78

Etherington, NA: 43, 45, 47-48

Goba, B: 76, 78, 85
Gqubule, Simon: 28, 63, 82-83

Hastings, Adrian: 21, 29
Healing/illness: 36, 45, 50-51
Hermeneutics: 21, 72-79, 86, 89*n9*, 90*n11*, 114

Jabavu, DDT: 3-4, 5, 8-9

King, Martin Luther: 17, 59
Kraft, C: 35-36
Kurewa, Z: 24

Legida, SP: 27-28
Liberation: 21, 39, 80
    of the poor and oppressed: 75, 80-82, 85-86, 88, 103, 106
    of the black masses: 23*n14*
Liberation theology:
    Latin America: 9, 19-22, 23*n18*, 71, 74, 80, 86, 93*n64*, 111
    South Africa: 14, 20, 22*n1*, 71-93, 89*n2*, 111, 113-114
Loewan, Jacob: 51-52
Luthuli, Albert John: 3-5, 8-10

Mabona, M: 29
Maimela, S: 84, 89*n2*, 92*n58*
Makhaye, M: 36
Matthews, ZK: 3-5
Mbiti, John: 18-19, 101
Mgojo, E: 63, 77-79
Missionaries: 1-2, 30-34, 43, 46-49, 103
Moore, B: 61, 72, 80, 89*n5*, 100-101
Mosothoane, EK: 35, 76-78, 81
Mpunzi, A: 79

Nederduitse Gereformeerde Kerk (NGK): 2-3, 83, 94-96, 98-99, 105, 114
Nederduitse Gereformeerde Kerk in Afrika (NGKA): 2, 83
Nederduitse Gereformeerde Sendingkerk/Sendingkerk (NGSK): 2, 83
Nationalism:
    Afrikaner: 6, 66, 83, 106-7*n1*
    Black: 11, 53, 65-68, 80, 85, 111
    African: 3, 15

National Conference of Black Churchmen (NCBC): 17
Nxumalo, JA: 30-31

Oosthuizen, GC: 49

Pato, Luke: 31-33
Pityane, N: 65
Pobee, John S: 14-15
Pretorius, Hennie: 70*n30*, 99-100

Reformed Church of Africa (RCA): 2, 83
Reconciliation: 17, 65-67, 70*n32*, 83, 103, 111, 113

South African Council of Churches (SACC): 83, 95-97
South African Student Organisation (SASO): 59, 60-61, 75
Sebidi, LJ: 35, 37
Serote, SE: 30
Setiloane, Gabriel M: 27-28, 35, 102
Shuuya, IK: 27
Steyn, MT, Chairman of the Committee of Inquiry into the Mass Media (1982): 101-102
Sundkler, Bengt: 43-45, 49-51
Syncretism: 37, 43, 49-52, 57*n38*, 112

Tile, Nehemiah: 44, 46, 55*n7*
Turner, HW: 44, 49-50
Tutu, Desmond: 18, 25-26, 30, 36-37, 81, 84, 101-102

University Christian Movement (UCM): 60-61

Vundla, Philip Qipu: 7-8

World Alliance of Reformed Churches (WARC): 83
West, M: 44-46, 50-51
Wilmore, Gayraud S: 17, 59
Women: 54, 57*n51*, 74, 84, 92*n57*

Yoder, John H: 86-87

Zulu, Alpheus: 9, 10-12, 81